M000083246

Culture–Sensitive Ministry
HELPFUL STRATEGIES FOR PASTORAL MINISTERS

Kenneth McGuire, CSP
Eduardo Fernández, SJ
Anne Hansen

Paulist Press
New York/Mahwah, NJ

The Scripture quotations contained herein are from the New Revised Standard Version: Catholic Edition Copyright © 1989 and 1993, by the Division of Christian Education of the National Council of the Churches of Christ in the United States of America. Used by permission. All rights reserved.

Cover and book design by Lynn Else

Copyright © 2010 by Paulist Press, Inc.

All rights reserved. No part of this book may be reproduced or transmitted in any form or by any means, electronic or mechanical, including photocopying, recording, or by any information storage and retrieval system without permission in writing from the Publisher.

Library of Congress Cataloging-in-Publication Data

McGuire, Kenneth.
    Culture-sensitive ministry : helpful strategies for pastoral ministers / Kenneth McGuire, Eduardo Fernández, Anne Hansen.
        p. cm.
    ISBN 978-0-8091-4651-2 (alk. paper)
    1. Pastoral theology. 2. Multiculturalism—Religious aspects—Christianity. I. Fernández, Eduardo C. II. Hansen, Anne, 1947– III. Title.
    BV4011.3.M34 2010
    253.089—dc22

                                                                              2009047355

Published by Paulist Press
997 Macarthur Boulevard
Mahwah, New Jersey 07430

www.paulistpress.com

Printed and bound in the
United States of America

Contents

(Complete set of handouts available at:
http://www.paulistpress.com/Culture-Sensitive_Ministry.html)

Acknowledgments

First of all, we want to thank and acknowledge the contributions of all those who have participated in our workshops. At this point they number over eight hundred people. Their experience and evaluations have helped us focus, refine, and prioritize the work.

We thank those who have read and critiqued various parts and versions of the manuscript: Bill Edens, CSP, and Brett Hoover, CSP. We also express our gratitude to Ron Hansen for his patience during the many hours of manuscript preparation.

Our appreciation goes to Sr. Caridad Inda, CHM, and to Louie Velasquez for their Spanish translations of the various hand-outs. We also thank Brett Hoover, CSP, for his aid in compiling the latest list of resources.

We thank the president of Paulist Press, Rev. Larry Boadt, CSP, for his encouragement of this project. We acknowledge the valuable assistance and suggestions from our editor at Paulist Press, Rev. Michael Kerrigan, CSP.

We also appreciate the support of Robert Hurteau, PhD, of the Center for Religion and Spirituality at Loyola Marymount University in Los Angeles.

And finally, we, the authors, would like to acknowledge each other's unique contributions. Our time together—writing, editing, and rewriting the final version of the manuscript—was not always easy but it was ultimately worthwhile, both professionally and personally. We did our best to put into practice what we have been trying to portray in our lives of ministry: teaching, writing, and giving workshops

Preview

The twenty-first century is full of challenges and changes: global, local, political, economic, and religious. Diverse cultures are living, worshipping, and working side by side. We can lament and wait for someone or some organization to address the challenges, or we can read the signs of the times, roll up our sleeves, and get to work.

Within the Church, record numbers of laypeople are seeking knowledge and expertise in theology and ministry. Their search reflects a desire to live out baptismal rights and duties that embody the good news. As laypeople move into roles of greater responsibility of leadership within the Church, there is an obligation to offer skills and strategies that will insure a higher degree of success in bringing the diverse cultures of their communities together.

The culture of the United States is famous for the idea that anyone with a sense of determination and the willingness to work hard can be successful. Regardless of the truth of this belief, stories abound that seem to affirm the possibility. We suggest it is time to adopt this can-do attitude and begin to address cultural sensitivity in our church, parish, and school settings, all the while remembering that cultural sensitivity includes more than ethnic and racial differences. It also involves issues of age, social class, gender, sexual orientation, disabilities, and marital status, among others.

This book is filled with motivational tips and concrete suggestions for ministers. It is a process book, not a traditional text book. It is more about a way of being and doing, a manner of listening and discussing, rather than about the acquisition of a set of defined knowledge. For whatever topics that a particular group wants to explore, we suggest, based on our experience, to begin by discovering the information and wisdom already present in the group.

Throughout the book, you will find suggestions for the process. As a way to engage further in this dynamic, interactive process, additional online resources and handouts are available and may be accessed by going to http://www.paulistpress.com/Culture-Sensitive _Ministry.html. These handouts serve as a summary of the topic and perhaps fill in some gaps or give some specific word or phrases to aid further understanding and discussion.

We call this the *"learning as you go"* process. Periodically and consistently throughout the discussions, we suggest that you pose the question "What have I learned?" to yourself and those who participate in your groups. As students, we are our best teachers.

We challenge you to dig into and reflect on your own experiences and those of your coministers. Mine the wisdom already present and then use the handouts as summary reflections for final discussions. You will be surprised at the results.

Culture-sensitive ministry is a powerful community-building approach to gather wisdom and develop confidence; it can also be fun as well as challenging work.

Take the opportunity to use this book. Don't let God's challenge and this opportunity pass you by.

PART ONE

The Motivation

1
What's This All About?
AN OVERVIEW

"…for I was hungry and you gave me food, I was thirsty and you gave me something to drink, I was a stranger and you welcomed me."

Matthew 25:35

INTRODUCTION

The past three decades have seen a massive growth in ethnic and cultural diversity throughout the United States and within the Catholic Church. Individuals move away from their native lands, from state to state, from profession to profession, and from group to group, for various and sundry reasons. They move in search of adventure, a more peaceful way of life, or freedom and prosperity for themselves and their families. The Catholic Church welcomes people from all over the world into its many parishes, agencies, and institutions. While this welcome is often genuine, it presents challenges for parish life: How does a parish welcome and integrate people with their gifts, talents, and cultural differences into our existing communities?

It is time to see and hear differently, to speak and act differently. It is time to lead the way in bringing cultures together. We cannot afford cultural illiteracy in the Catholic Church, or in society for that matter. If we make the changes to bridge cultural boundaries, we will not only be helping those who come to us from other countries, we will be a role model for society at large, bringing religion into the public square, exactly where it is needed to promote the common good.

The focus in this book is to persuade and encourage parish communities to look at the challenge of cultural diversity and pray for the courage to embrace it. We will then become models for society in the true way that Jesus instructed in the Gospels, specifically in the Beatitudes. We will be the consolers, the peacemakers, the seekers of justice, and the caregivers of the poor in both body and spirit. We will be a force that works, above all, to bring people of the world together as fellow human beings rather than as members of opposing countries, clans, or tribes.

The following examples offer a glimpse into the lives of people who have crossed cultural borders. Their stories will be repeated many times in our parishes, schools, and institutions. Are we prepared to welcome them?

A priest from Ghana comes to Los Angeles to begin classes at a Catholic university in pursuit of a graduate degree in pastoral theology, which will give him skills to help his fellow Catholics in Africa. He is assigned to an affluent, bustling parish that will be his home while in school.

☉

A family of six relocates from Boston to Los Angeles due to the career advances of the parents. The four children, used to the Catholic school system, are enrolled in public school and must attend religious education classes at their new parish.

☉

A nun from Vietnam, now in a southern California parish, struggles to choose the correct phrase in English to explain her ideas about teaching religious education.

☉

A young man from Croatia marries a woman from California and moves to Los Angeles with her, involving himself in the church and community.

☉

A couple nearing retirement moves to another part of the city and into a new parish. Their years of service in their former parish are left behind as they start over.

◯

A woman from Guatemala immigrates to the United States and secures a job as a receptionist at a Catholic church. She is a single mother with three children in need of schooling and sacramental preparation.

◯

A family of five emigrates from Pakistan to escape the violence that is affecting their children. They leave behind elderly parents, siblings, and cousins, as well as a home that took them years to establish. They hope to bring other family members to the United States in the future. Their welcome is not as warm as anticipated due to the backlash from the terrorist attacks of September 11, 2001.

◯

A new college graduate gets a great job that requires moving to a strange city many miles from his hometown. Realizing he knows no one and looking to make connections, he attends the local Catholic church. After a few months he wonders if he is even welcome. He is gay.

In addition to these people, there are hundreds of thousands who come from other countries to escape the desperation of poverty and violence. These immigrants need and deserve respect for the cultural differences they bring with them to this country, as they work to integrate into the mainstream of American life.

This book is for all those who work with such groups as immigrants, as mentioned above, or with professionals following job opportunities, senior citizens relocating, college students moving to campuses, families making new beginnings, or people coming together as nontraditional families. This book will help the parish that wants to approach ministry and parish life from an intercultural and intergenerational model where all groups and subgroups work and live together. The material is not about becoming a master at understanding culture or of crossing cultural boundaries. It is a practical approach to coming together and meshing in faith, culture, and understanding. It is meant for the parish or organization that seeks to build an inclusive community welcoming all of God's people.

The first part of the book is motivational, meant to inspire the reader, just as the picture of a chocolate cake in a recipe book inspires the baker to follow the recipe. The latter section of the book can be viewed as the owner's manual—the recipe for success running workshops. They describe the process for use of space, time, and talents in the workshop settings. They are "the guts" of the book because it is from these chapters that the reader will learn how to confidently lead a workshop on cultural diversity—a workshop with the potential to transform the participants as well as the agencies they represent.

The final chapter summarizes the authors' experiences, successes, and ideas for growth. It would be beneficial to first read the book through to gain an overall picture, and then go back and concentrate on one chapter at a time. It is our hope that the reader will be as challenged and energized as we have been.

All three of the authors recognize the urgent need to bring this program to parish communities. Two of the authors have been doing cultural orientation workshops with foreign-born priests and nuns for more than ten years; the other has spent over fifteen years teaching bereavement ministry in numerous parishes. They have seen firsthand the need for cultural awareness and understanding. In this book, they will share their experiences, their ideas, and their model for running workshops on cultural bridge-building. While the authors do not claim to have the only method or format, they have been very successful in their work with foreign-born ministers. Participant evaluations validate this claim and have encouraged them to share their efforts with a broader community.

The feelings of the participants, submitted anonymously in written evaluations after the workshops have ended, express self-affirmation, a sense of being understood, a recognition that horizons have been broadened, and a growing desire to be more compassionate toward those with differing backgrounds and personal experiences. In the throes of culture shock many of those who attend the workshops arrived critical of others, U.S. society, and themselves. The orientation to cultural dynamics in the context of faith-sharing that is offered in these workshops has helped them understand that the problems often do not lie in persons but in cultural misunderstandings. Comments such as the following one are common: *"Now I see why people are like they are in the United States. It's not necessarily that they are secularized, but in fact they have been living their faith in ways I had not noticed or understood."*

There are many ways to live out one's faith, and those ways are culturally influenced. This book is intended to help parishes understand this idea and then work with the cultural differences that exist in their communities, benefiting everyone, the established parishioner as well as the newcomer. As later chapters will note, cultural differences are not only about ethnicity but also about our membership in groups and subgroups.

The study of culture is a rather young science and its far-reaching effects are just beginning to be grasped. A massive cultural literacy program is needed, and this book is a step in that direction. It is the result of many years of work and experience with a great variety of people in workshops, retreats, and other pastoral settings. The catalyst for writing this book is the need for cultural understanding at the parish level for everyone. The Cultural Orientation Program for International Ministers (COPIM) has a workshop template that offers a methodology for bridging gaps in parishes.

The bishops of the United States are concerned about the ethnic and cultural diversity in the American Church and hope more attention will be paid to integration without total assimilation—cultural blending without losing one's own sense of culture. It should be noted that at this point in time, the notion of integration without assimilation may be countercultural and is not a popular concept with some citizens and politicians who want anyone living in America to forsake their country of origin. This makes the work of cultural awareness and acceptance even more important.

Loyola Marymount University's decision to involve more people in these types of workshops provided the final push in the efforts to bring this book to fruition. It was in working with various levels of the Church that we realized there was a need for this type of learning.

The nuanced understanding of the dynamics of culture and faith formation that lead to transformation will benefit ministry within the Church, as well as in schools, in professional lives, in politics, and in neighborhoods. The more people understand each other, the better it is for society in general.

THE AUTHORS

The authors, while all from the United States, have different backgrounds and areas of expertise. Each brings a special sensitivity to the topic of cultural diversity and the importance of understanding it in the modern church setting. Ken McGuire and Eduardo Fernández are both Catholic priests; Ken is a Paulist Father and Eduardo, a Jesuit. Anne Hansen is a writer specializing in family and ministry issues. Each has crossed cultural borders over the span of their own life experiences, which gives each of them an understanding of the subject.

Ken was raised on a farm, where he learned the skills of living in rural middle-America. He was the first in his family to attend college, which was a major crossing of cultural boundaries, from rural life to city life and then to that of higher education. This led him to a master's degree in the study of botany and farm crops. At age twenty-three, Ken crossed another important boundary. He had been raised as a nonpracticing Protestant, but during high school years had tried out several churches, including the Methodist Church, the Lutheran Church, and the Church of Jesus Christ of the Latter Day Saints. He converted to Catholicism and eventually took this conversion to ordination to the priesthood. In the middle of this Ken continued his education, receiving another master's degree, this time in theology. Eventually, in an attempt to merge his divergent fields of formal study, these degrees led him to a PhD in cultural anthropology.

Eduardo's life also exhibits several patterns of crossing cultural boundaries. Born five minutes from the United States–Mexican border in El Paso, Texas, to second-generation Mexican American parents, he quickly learned that there was more than one "correct" way of doing things and seeing the world. A cradle Catholic, he attended a small parochial school staffed by nuns from the United States, Ireland, and Mexico. Jesuits from Mexico staffed his local parish. At the age of eighteen, he underwent his first experience of culture shock when he left his hometown to study sociology in New Orleans. How could two neighboring states, Texas and Louisiana, be so different? After graduating from college with a degree in sociology, he experienced another culture shock when he joined the Jesuit novitiate in Grand Coteau, Louisiana. He went on to receive a master's in Latin American Studies and, after earning the requisite MDiv in theology, sought to integrate his previous studies, successfully combining the social sciences with theology. A licentiate and doctorate in missiology, which focuses on the relationship between faith and culture, gave him that opportunity. Travels for study and ministry to various locations in Texas, Florida, California, Mexico, and finally Rome, Italy, each brought its own cultural challenges. He recalls a friend's remark, which he understood only years later: "You have studied in both Berkeley and Rome, each thinking that it is the center of the universe!"

Anne Hansen grew up in a large Irish Italian Catholic family and graduated from college with a degree in psychology. She married and experienced her first cultural crossing when she moved to Phoenix, Arizona, with a baby in hand and one on the way. Like Eduardo, she could not understand how two neighboring states, in this case California and Arizona, could be so different. After the birth of her fourth child, she moved to Ireland with her husband and children. It was definitely a culture shock that took about six months to work through before the experience was appreciated. Living in a foreign land and adapting to the different lifestyle, educational system, and social system were each cultural boundary crossings. Upon returning to the United States, she gave birth to her fifth child, and then finished a master's degree in educational psychology, using the Irish experience as a point of study.

Anne went on to teach parenting classes and then took that experience to another level when she began writing a column for the Catholic press on family life and ministry. Her topics were varied, but they often focused on the antics and experiences of her five children. Each time one would go off to college, all in different parts of the country, there would be a new culture for that child to learn.

A number of years ago her brother contracted AIDS and died within three years of the diagnosis. She set off to learn as much as possible about the disease and what she could do to help those living and dying with it. She also embraced the gay community in respect for her deceased brother. These were certainly boundaries that required careful crossing. Today, she continues to write and is combining her ministry experience with her degrees in psychology by working toward a master's in pastoral theology.

IN CLOSING

Much of our experience has come from using the Cultural Orientation Program for International Ministers (COPIM) at Loyola Marymount University. This program serves as an excellent model for raising cultural awareness in parishes, schools, the business community, and other institutions. There is no limit as to where this program can be used. Its basic premise, that being aware of our own culture as well as that of another's will ultimately bring a greater understanding among people, is simple yet profound. It is an awareness that has the remarkable potential to change the climate of the parish, the school, or the office.

The main focus of this book, although again not the only focus, is that cross-cultural ministry merits special attention. From diocesan centers to parish centers, the need to develop an awareness of cultural diversity is crucial. Those who become involved in this important work will be bridge-builders across cultural borders. The skills and insights gained from the precepts of this program will translate from church work and ministry into society at large and has the potential to bring about positive change in the way human beings respond and react to each other.

The challenge is immense. It can be feared due to the apprehension that change sometimes brings, or it can welcomed— embraced wholeheartedly with the understanding that it is a new

Pentecost, opening up the possibility of inspiring relationships, gifts, and alternatives.

We can be receptive to an increasing multiculturalism with all its hopes and joys, or we can deny it, trying to stem the tide of change. Neither option affects the reality that this era of multiculturalism has arrived. How we, as a Church, choose to deal with it is the question.

QUESTIONS FOR REFLECTION AND DISCUSSION

1. Do you have a story to tell about moving from one culture to another?
2. Is your parish up to the challenge of reading the signs of the times and embracing diverse cultures?

FOR FURTHER REFLECTION

"There is being constructed a sign...which enables all humans to dwell together with each other as enriching each other and enabling each other to share God's life and God's goodness starting now." James Alison, *Undergoing God: Dispatches from the Scene of a Break-in* (New York: Continuum, 2006), 77–78.

2
The Complexity of Culture

Let mutual love continue. Do not neglect to show hospi-
tality to strangers, for by doing that some have entertained
angels without knowing it.

Hebrews 13:1–2

In this era of globalization the understanding of culture has emerged as a critical issue. The understanding starts with one's own culture and moves to those cultures with which one interacts. For many, this moving beyond the comfort zone of their own culture is a threat, a difficult move. To facilitate the movement, ministers will need special skills of patience, acceptance, and the ability to draw forth stories from both the new and the established parishioner or community member.

Recognizing, understanding, and accepting cultural differences is imperative. No parish, institution, or organization is mono-cultural. Every community is made up of groups: teenagers, young adults, seniors, college students, and parents, to name a few. Each subgroup or subculture inhabits a different part of the larger cul-ture, and each group has beliefs, needs, and ideas on how things are to be best accomplished.

While most of us think of cultural boundaries as being about ethnicity, they also include the subcultures of age, gender, family structure, educational background, socioeconomic level, and sex-ual orientation, among others.

In the changing Church and the mobile society of today, people move freely from one side of the world to another. All min-isters in today's Church face a multicultural reality. If pastoral service is going to be effective, every parish has to work to clarify and understand its own cultural and subcultural boundaries.

Despite the fact that the United States has always been a land of immigrants, the ethnic landscape of this country has changed dramatically since the 1960s. In addition, the American cultural landscape has changed. The rise of feminism, the influence of the "me" generation, significant changes in dress codes, the acknowledgment of sexual diversity, and an increasing tolerance for differences bring with them new viewpoints and a need for greater understanding.

Immigrants from all over the world have come here to live, create communities, and integrate themselves into the civic and religious social order. Yet, many are still looked upon as different, and in some cases are feared, due to the political circumstances of the time.

When immigrants join a parish community, their languages, customs, and styles of ministry can conflict with the expected order of business. To properly prepare people for ministry in the United States and to support their work with diverse segments of the modern Church means teaching as much as possible about the many cultures that are represented in our urban and suburban parishes, schools, and other organizations. This includes not only the immigrants that come through the door each year but various other groups: youth, seniors, families of all kinds of makeup, traditional and single-parent families, working parents, the divorced and separated, singles, and any other group identified within the parish, school, or organization.

Sometimes this will require a stretch in personal perceptions of who belongs and who does not, and it is precisely at that point the information contained in this book will prove invaluable. Following the teachings of Jesus calls for the recognition that all are welcome.

As dioceses and parishes experience the arrival of priests and nuns from other countries coming to live and work in the United States Church, it becomes crucial that these new arrivals are assisted in acquiring the skills of proclaiming the gospel and sharing the teachings of the Church beyond their own culture. While many of these priests and religious are present to serve immigrants to this country in their native language, they must also understand and minister to the needs of people who have been living in the U.S. culture for many years or who are native to the country. As this takes place, established parishioners benefit by becoming more aware of their own culture and by recognizing that the priest is another representative of cultural diversity in the Catholic Church.

The same can be said about the newly welcomed immigrants as they assimilate into their new surroundings. These immigrants want to be married in the Church, have their children baptized and their dead buried, as well as have their lives enriched with spiritual guidance and leadership that addresses their specific cultural system. The coming together of foreign-born ministers, immigrant populations, and native-born and naturalized Americans presents a remarkable opportunity for a broader, more open Catholic Church.

While exciting, this mingling of cultures is also challenging and brings with it people and ideas that complicate civil and Church life. This complication of life is not a negative but rather an opportunity to view parish tradition and determine if some change is necessary. As far as the Church is concerned, the viewing of tradition now has to come through global eyes, noting that there is not one way to worship, participate in liturgy, or belong to a Catholic community. The myriad of cultures now present in the Church of the United States offers opportunity for an evolution and shift in how things are done, creating better understanding and cooperation. Each culture, while retaining its own identity, will contribute to a broadening, universalizing (catholicizing) of the local Church and culture of the country.

Those already in ministry have the greatest responsibility to share their knowledge and experience as well as to learn as much as they can about other cultures. It certainly is not just a case of foreigners coming to the United States and picking up "North American ways." It is sharing and respecting the established traditions, as well as deciding to learn the ways of new arrivals.

This meeting, sharing, and exchanging cultural information have the benefit of helping learners see and understand their own culture more clearly. In learning and sharing, all cultures will gain affirmation. The question is: Can we learn to appreciate that more than one way of life is not only possible, but also acceptable and good? This is a challenge that has to be explored, discussed honestly and openly, and then addressed by entire communities. The significance of this challenge is immense and ultimately life changing.

Again, reiterating a significant point: It is important to remember that most people think of a different culture as "those people over there," from other countries and other ethnic backgrounds. In reality, cultural differences are defined far beyond geographical borders. For example, cultural boundaries and differences are clearly visible in the religious views held between generations within the United States. Within every parish are those who are uncomfortable with post–Vatican II thinking and those who embrace it, which thus makes the work of learning how to cross cultural boundaries advantageous for parish councils, liturgy, and social-service committees, and parishioners of every age level, from schoolchildren to seniors. The future of every parish will include recognizing more and more multicultural needs.

Participating in the process of sharing cultural backgrounds and stories is what will bind the culturally diverse parish community together. As people learn to listen to each other, they will begin to respect themselves and each other with a new level of excitement. They will begin to understand that differences, while seemingly monumental, are often simply differences of language, food, and tradition. They will also learn that their similarities—kind, caring hearts that are searching for peace, a sense of belonging, and faith in God—draw them together far more than their differences draw them apart.

In this era of worldwide cultural clashes, it becomes even more important for the Catholic Church to lead the way to bringing cultures together to recognize their shared humanity and then, from this recognition, to empower them to deeper levels of ministry—ministries that, like those of the Master, welcome the stranger, console the afflicted, and reconcile the outcast.

QUESTIONS FOR REFLECTION AND DISCUSSION

1. Am I aware of the different cultures in my (parish) community?
2. Am I open to listening to the life experiences and explanations of traditions from those of a culture other than my own?
3. Can I name three areas in my parish community where the need for cultural awareness would benefit it?
4. How prepared am I to stretch my thinking on who belongs and who does not belong?

FOR FURTHER REFLECTION

"People who turn you off, people you're afraid of, have a message for you....They're triggering something within you. You need them." Richard Rohr, *Radical Grace: Daily Meditations* (Cincinnati: St. Anthony Messenger Press, 1995), 182.

3
A Bird's-Eye View of Culture

Let us then pursue what makes for peace and mutual upbuilding."

Romans 14:19

DEFINITIONS

What is culture? One clear, concise version is that culture is simply the sum total of our nonbiological inheritance. Culture is that part of life concerned with a people's appearance, the effects of their environment, their tools for work, their material goods, their communal organization, and their thoughts about themselves and the world. Culture is the human way of making meaning out of life. Human beings look to their families, clans, tribes, or nations to help them figure out this meaning—and have been doing so since the beginning of time. Every new experience requires integration into and understanding within the culture. Humans seek meaning from the wisdom of those who have gone before them, from traditions, science, and personal insights, as well as from the insights of others.

Crossing cultural boundaries is a natural and commonplace occurrence in everyone's life. Sometimes the crossing is simple, hardly noticed, such as a move across town. At other times, such as a move to another state or country, the crossing can be complicated and difficult. It always takes time, effort, and work to adapt to and become comfortable in another culture, and the experience deserves to be recognized and considered for the consequences it brings.

There is a long-standing argument, familiar to many and still waged today, over the influences of *nature* (genetics) versus *nurture* (culture). As it turns out, both play a big part in human development. Coping with life involves coping with genetic inheritance and inherited culture. Making sense out of the meshing of the two is what makes each individual unique. No human being exists without culture. It is something carried within each individual from birth to death and influences far more of life than most realize.

Humans are formed twice—initially by genetics and then by culture. These effects begin at birth and continue throughout life. Genes and culture are indelible characteristics carried from birth to the grave. Everyone can cite examples where genetics have been a factor in their life. Genetics play a part in physical characteristics, such as baldness, and in health, such as family disposition to breast or prostate cancer. It contributes to sexual orientation. Also, alcoholism and some forms of mental illness are said to be genetically influenced.

Culture affects life in the same way. The food that is eaten and enjoyed, the clothes that are worn, the religious practices that are preferred, and the holiday traditions that have meaning are all greatly determined by culture. They become a part of a person, just as their blue or brown eyes are a part of them.

Culture consists of the discreet social interactions of people between each other, their environment, and their technology. Culture is constructed from the whole social consensus a group: what it is, how it acts, how it thinks, and which subgroups and individuals are part of it. It includes the conscious and the unconscious, the reflective and the unreflective, and many of the behavior choices and automatic reactions individuals exhibit.

Culture is not a God-given feature bestowed on a certain group of people. Culture is a system naturally created by a group of people, making choices both individually and collectively. These choices over time are integrated into the group and either become part of the culture or are discarded as unnecessary or hazardous. For example, it is particularly "American" to be independent and to have the ability to "pull yourself up by the bootstraps." American culture is built on the belief that anyone who works hard enough can realize the American dream of home ownership and wealth. Whether or not this is true for all Americans is another story; the belief has evolved as part of the culture of the United States.

Making meaning of life is crucial to human survival. A mistake in an outsider's reading of meaning in a culture will result in a mistake in communicating with that culture. At worst, this can lead to conflict and even war. On a smaller scale it leads to confusion and misunderstanding, which in turn leave individuals feeling alienated.

CROSSING CULTURAL BOUNDARIES

Individuals may physically move to another culture and, over a period of time, adopt the ways of the culture in which they are living. Even then, however, they never forget the original way they lived, behaved, ate, or celebrated. A basic example of crossing a cultural boundary can be explained by looking at what happens when two people get married. Each partner comes to the marriage with a certain culture, a certain way of living. The cultures they bring together may be similar or very different. The more different they are, the more adjustments will need to be made by each partner. Even if both grew up celebrating holidays in a similar fashion, they will have differences when it comes to important holidays, such as Christmas. These differences usually emerge when the couple have children and begin to develop their traditions. One spouse may come from a family that wrapped each gift elaborately and arranged them under the Christmas tree for the children to open on Christmas morning, with the idea that Santa left the gifts the night before. The other spouse may come from a family that scattered unwrapped gifts throughout the living room with the same idea of Santa leaving them the night before. In the case of some cultures, a Santa may not even be involved.

The expectation of how to handle the tradition of Christmas gifts is simple but can have a profound influence on the relationship. One partner has to forgo his or her cultural experience and move to a new way of doing things. This means giving up a bit of one's own culture, which is never easy.

Parishes are also affected by culture—their own and that of their priests and ministers. When foreign priests and nuns come to the United States to minister, bringing with them a bit of their native culture, it can be uncomfortable for the parish.

The American parish has existed in various forms for many years. As might be expected, each parish becomes accustomed to conducting things in its own way. To change after many years is not an easy task. People have preferences in terms of style of liturgy, priorities of parish ministry, and various ideas on parish governing structure. The introduction of a foreign minister can be disconcerting to some and requires sensitivity both for the parishioners and the new minister.

Priests all over the world progress through seminary education and training to ordination predisposed to a certain set of cultural expectations. In some regions of the world the parish priest has the final word on decisions concerning the parish community. So there is quite an adjustment that has to take place before this foreign-born, foreign-educated priest can be completely comfortable with the structure of parishes in the United States, which calls for certain decisions to be made together with parish councils and lay staffs. Both the parish culture and the culture of the foreign minister have to be considered, with each side making an effort to spend time learning about and understanding each other.

The phenomenon also takes place within the parish community at large. Longtime parishioners are comfortable with the way things are done and business is conducted. Young adults, the children of the long-established parishioners, are often bored, wanting to modernize the community so it can be, in their view, up to speed with contemporary society. This cycle is repeated generation after generation, in parish after parish.

The same can be said for any immigrant coming to America. Despite the universality of the Catholic liturgy there are regional differences. For example, the mode of acceptable dress differs from region to region. It could be shocking to attend Mass at a Catholic church in the United States for the first time and see somewhat scantily clad young girls and women receiving holy communion, or to see eucharistic ministers wearing jeans and sandals. To the new immigrant, this style of dress might be viewed as a sign of disrespect. In the United States, geography, weather conditions, and fashion often dictate the type of clothes worn, whereas, in other parts of the world, dress codes are often more formal and traditional.

On a recent trip to Florence, Italy, coauthor Anne Hansen experienced a cultural crossing involving dress that caused her to balk and initially refuse to accept the boundary. She was visiting the beautiful church of Santa Maria Novella, accompanied by her sister. The two women, one in her forties and the other in her fifties were dressed conservatively in skirts and T-shirts appropriate to the warm weather. After paying to enter the church, they were approached by a docent and instructed to cover themselves with a piece of dark material. A sign at the door had informed them that shorts were not acceptable and they joked that at their ages shorts were never acceptable. However, they did notice that most of the men entering the church were wearing shorts, again due to the very warm weather, and that these men were not offered the dark piece of material to cover themselves. Anne put the fabric loosely around her shoulders and proceeded to view the artwork around the church. Within a few minutes the docent crossed the huge expanse of the church with what appeared to be a guard. Anne was told to put the fabric on to completely cover her bare shoulders or to leave the church. It was a difficult moment. There was no explanation and both women were stunned. They complied but after a few minutes left the church, knowing they would not return. They were angry.

Once outside of the church they approached the docents and guards and asked questions about the placement of the Blessed Sacrament. They were informed it was on the other side of the site in a private chapel. Ironically, there were no dress restrictions posted by the door of that chapel. The women calmly questioned the policy and were simply told it was the way it was done. Later, over coffee, they talked about the difficulty of being in a culture that was different and to them unreasonable. They concluded that, while they did not in any way agree with the policy, they understood it was a product of the culture and not theirs to question at that time.

What is accepted with few questions in Italy, Mexico, or the Philippines may be unacceptable in the United States (and vice versa, of course), and figuring out all of this can be a daunting task for the newcomer. It is not a case of right or wrong; it is a case of what one is used to and what one has lived with, usually since childhood.

In other parts of the world, where a feudal system of class distinction or even remnants of a caste system remain, it is difficult to imagine the ability of the average person to move out of his or her "designated" group. While this is difficult for Americans to understand, it must be respected and taken into account when individuals from these cultures come to the United States.

Each culture makes decisions and then lives with those decisions for generations, until they are proven no longer true. As explained above, this is evidenced by the dress restrictions placed on women entering a church in Europe. Despite the sexualization of society, with billboards and buses adorned with nearly naked women, it is still the norm in many countries that even conservatively dressed women with only an arm exposed are stopped and asked to cover themselves. Culture does not always make sense for those outside the culture.

Just as Anne and her sister did not understand or agree with the notion that their aging, barely exposed arms needed to be covered to enter a church in Italy, immigrant people have to deal with what one might categorize as scandalous dress codes here in the United States. Adapting to another culture is at times difficult, even demoralizing.

Coping with life involves coping with genetic inheritance and inherited meaning, which together is culture. Making sense out of the seeming chaos of experience is a lifetime struggle for individuals, groups, and cultures. Being human means always asking why. On a cultural level, they ask: "Why does she like that kind of food?"…"Why does he act like that?"…"Why do they dress like that?" On a more scientific level, human beings question where the birds are going when they fly a certain way, how the sun works, and why the seasons change. They are forever looking for answers, the meaning of things that they experience.

Immigrants from Mexico expect the rituals of mourning a loved one to proceed in a certain way, with a certain style and color of clothing. They expect specific religious rituals and, without these rituals, feel their loved one is not being mourned properly, creating more grief for them. The Irish expect something different, and then there are those who do not request any type of memorial service for their deceased. Everyone comes to these expectations due to their cultural experiences, and if people do not understand each other's customs and cultures, they can omit important rituals or even worse ignore or ridicule native cultural practices.

CONCLUSIONS

It is imperative for religious professionals and parish staffs they work with to recognize the importance of cultural expectations when it comes to the landmark events of life such as baptisms, weddings, and funerals. These moments of meaning for individuals and families are recognized as moments of true evangelization. However, if cultural preferences are ignored or dismissed, the moments of evangelization can become meaningless, negative, and even bitter reminders of a Church failing its task.

Again, the purpose of the material in this book is to emphasize that those who cross cultural boundaries will have to cope with different cultural expectations. They will have to learn new ways of doing things, and it will take a great deal of patience and sensitivity on the part of those involved in ministry.

It is especially important that our churches welcome, embrace, teach, and learn from those who are joining us from abroad. In a country such as ours, which has a history of legal discrimination against people with darker skin and is currently dealing with acrimonious debate over passing immigration laws and profiling individuals for their potential as terrorists, it becomes a task of education as well as one of raising awareness. It will be important to use the life and words of Jesus to help some in the church communities recognize that being of a different culture is not something to be feared. We will have to actively model and talk about the inclusiveness of Jesus, especially for the poor and the marginalized.

QUESTIONS FOR REFLECTION AND DISCUSSION

1. Have I ever felt confused, perhaps even angry, when I had to cross a cultural boundary?
2. Is my parish open to integrating the traditions of the many cultures represented throughout it into the liturgies and other practices within the parish? If not, what can I do to facilitate a move in this direction?

FOR FURTHER REFLECTION

"Communities thrive when the insights, perspectives, and experiences of a broad base of the community are accessed and respected. A spirit of mutuality and collaboration serves as the foundation for this. The community gathers, not divided between 'those in the know' and 'the folks in the pew,' but as people journeying together toward becoming a more effective evangelizing force. The wisdom of all of the members is essential." Jane E. Regan, *Toward an Adult Church: A Vision of Faith Formation* (Chicago: Loyola Press, 2002), 165–66.

4

Culture: The Human Essential

Beloved, you do faithfully whatever you do for the friends,
even though they are strangers to you; they have testified to
your love before the church.

3 John 5–6

To be human is to be part of a culture. Humans are social beings born into groups where they live and struggle to survive. They cope with climate, manufacture tools, find food, and build shelters. Every human group, because of its culture, has a specific form of communication: spoken, written, and acted out through gestures.

Culture is such a part of life that it is "just common sense." Each individual is shaped by culture and in turn shapes the culture. Every culture has continuity and yet changes. (There are many ways that cultures change.) Culture provides "tool kits" or different skills that enable people to organize their experience and to cope with their environment.

Anthropology, the study of aspects of human life, tells us that all cultures have some form of origin story. Prior to modern science, it was accepted knowledge that all existing things had been brought into being by God (gods) and that everything had a specific place in the great hierarchy of being. Human interest in origins, relationships, and God (gods) has been evidenced wherever early human remains are discovered.

Myths and oral legends tell of human creation and the beginnings of various characteristics of a group's life as gifts or punishments from certain gods. Each cultural group's religious myths explain the story of their origin, and each group or culture emphasizes different things, although some stories share similar plots.

The cosmology of the universe, God, angels, humans, the universality of death, the social positions of men and women, and the need for constant hard work to maintain life are the major points of the myths (stories) that account for the human experience.

Human life seems to be organized on the basis of these stories, and it is these stories that serve as the foundations for the culture. For example, Christians look to Genesis to explain the story of Creation. Adam and Eve, Cain and Abel, and Noah and the Great Flood are carried from generation to generation, offering vivid descriptions of how life began and was organized. These ancient stories continue and culminate in the birth, death, and resurrection of Jesus Christ, as a model for moral living and for relating to the Creator, God. Every major religious group throughout the world has developed their own stories, often with amazing similarities. It is from these ancient stories that moral and legal codes come into existence and influence daily life.

Today, the concept of culture is used to describe how a certain group of people lives. For instance, the French, the Italians, and the Germans dress and prepare foods a certain way. We come to know what to expect of their customs, especially their culinary traits. We travel to China and come upon a French restaurant, knowing what the food will be. Crossing the bridges over the canals of Venice, Italy, we spot the golden arches of McDonald's and immediately understand that is an American symbol, and we know exactly what fare the restaurant offers.

It was not always this way. Generations ago people did not travel far from their places of birth. Today, due to technology, we can be 3000 miles from our home in a matter of hours. We eat breakfast in one time zone and dinner in another. Business is conducted in the morning in the Midwest and the businessperson returns to Los Angles by evening in time to attend a child's school function or a family dinner.

Technology, especially the use of the Internet, has helped the world become a sort of village with 24-hour communication possible to anyone, anywhere, if they have access to the Web. The implications for this are obvious. Young people in China and Africa can hear the music and see the fashions, movies, and television shows that young people in Europe and the United States experience. People can take classes from major universities while sitting in their living rooms.

The reality that communicating over the Internet allows individuals to be known only by screen names allows cultures that are vastly different from each other to communicate effectively. Language, accent, skin color, and style of dress are usually not known when one is communicating in cyberspace. In many ways this technology brings people's ideas together before the people actually meet. First impressions, which are often based primarily on what is seen, are eliminated in favor of conversation that is based on the pure sharing of ideas. It is a different world than it was thirty years ago, and with this has come a comingling of people and their traditions never imagined before. For some, the prospect of this comingling is exciting; for others it is threatening, giving way to fear that the way of life they have been used to (their culture) may be lost.

As we said earlier in chapter 3, culture is constructed from the whole social consensus of a group: what it is, how it acts, how it thinks, and which subgroups and individuals are part of it. These social subgroups are unique, each with its own story of who it is, where it came from, and what it is about.

Culture includes concepts of space, time, values, and beliefs. It is a blueprint for life in the group and has built-in control mechanisms. Each culture is an interpretive framework for making sense of the reality of the experiences of life. Each person in any given culture is uniquely different, even from others of the same culture, but they associate with each other and share certain self-identities; they take these associations and identities with them wherever they go.

For example, an American living abroad will seek out other Americans to celebrate July 4, Independence Day. It is a conscious act, but it is also somewhat automatic to want to be with other Americans on the day that independence is celebrated in the United States. The day is marked a success if the foods associated with July 4, such as hamburgers and hot dogs, potato salad, and chips are somehow available. The same thing happens in

November when it is Thanksgiving in America. Those living out of the country spend hours locating the things that made the holiday important and special for them when they were living in the United States. And, so it is with those who move to America. They find markets that carry their special foods and bookstores that carry newspapers and magazines in their language. They come together to celebrate their own national holidays specific to their culture. This is normal behavior. Cultures should be able to exist peacefully side by side, enjoying each other's traditions and customs.

However, as has happened in the history of the United States, as well as in other places across the world, there is a movement that insists people taking up residence in the country should shed their culture of origin, including their language, and assimilate completely into the new culture. What a shame if this were to happen! Cultures would grow static and suspicious, becoming more hostile to each other and less accepting of neighbors. The growth that brings about societal change would erode.

Every culture has varying groups within their culture. These groups are arranged by age, work, and economic or power status. This can be seen in every parish and diocese. Yet they will all identify as part of the whole culture. Occasionally, these subgroups may be sufficiently different as to be *recognized* as a subculture— New England culture, Southern culture, Church culture, or clerical culture. Each culture shapes its members and has structures and means for passing the culture onto the next generation. There is no escape from some form of social culture. It takes place even in our families, as is seen at family gatherings; the young, the old, the men, and the women tend to congregate in their own groups.

Each and every culture has pluses and minuses, costs and benefits. One culture is not superior to another. Each struggles to survive. Each has adapted to its specific climate, geography, and technology. These factors of climate, geography, and technology are not entirely under the control of the given culture, and one major climate change or civil unrest in a neighboring culture has great influence. Hurricane Katrina is an example of how a change in the "normal" climate can shift cultural emphasis.

It is important to remember and to infuse into ministry the idea that people coming from many different cultures have had different experiences with education and ministry. Their traditions, while sometimes similar, are for the most part different. The local Church needs to make a concerted effort to bring these people together and allow them to share their cultural experiences as they learn about and share in the culture of the local Church. Mutual respect will be beneficial to all, as each of the cultures explains and learns from each other. The challenge is that each culture will be modified. But this is part of the ever-changing face of culture. No culture remains static. This is clearly seen in generational shifts. Elders sometimes fear and are convinced that the culture is "falling apart," while the younger generation is impatient to "get away from the old rules" and embrace change.

This can be observed in the process of working with different groups in a parish. The personal stories of each individual and group are important. It is through the listening and sharing of stories that people will come together and learn about each other's cultures. That is what this book is about, developing a process for sharing, telling, and listening to individual and group stories.

It will be important that the parish, its people, and especially its pastors and ministers listen carefully to the explanations of the ways of life and the cultural experiences that others will bring to parishes and communities. An aura of caring for the individual will emerge by the very fact that others are listening. As newcomers share their life stories, they will be explaining their cultures with all its traditions. Listeners will come to understand what is important in the way of celebration, family, food, dress, worship, and education. There will be no forms to fill out, no format to follow. The simple sharing of the story will serve to educate others about the culture of the speaker.

QUESTIONS FOR REFLECTION AND DISCUSSION

1. What is your reaction to the idea that the comingling of cultures, generations, and social classes can cause concern, even a sense of being threatened, for some people?
2. Do you every worry that *your* culture may be lost one day?
3. What do you do to preserve your culture?

FOR FURTHER REFLECTION

"One of the least recognized gifts of the Spirit...may be what I will call the 'grace of self-doubt'...It is a grace that is accessible to those who struggle for understanding, those who have come to see things differently from what was once seen, those who have experienced the complexity of translating convictions into action." Margaret Farley, "Ethics, Ecclesiology, and the Grace of Self-Doubt," in *A Call to Fidelity: On the Moral Theology of Charles E. Curran*, eds. James J. Walter, Timothy E. O'Connell, and Thomas A. Shannon, (Washington, DC: Georgetown University Press, 2002), 66.

5

Types of Cultures and Their Characteristics

So then you are no longer strangers and aliens, but you are citizens with the saints and also members of the household of God.

Ephesians 2:19

Different types of cultures have been studied over the years and different characteristics have been categorized: for example, hunter-gatherers, pastoralists, slash-and-burn agriculturalists, urban dwellers, primitives, and peasants. Cultures have also been compared and contrasted over the last few decades. Several ways of relating these different cultures have been proposed but in recent decades the one most commonly used is the contrast between "traditional" and "modern" cultures. Very recently, a new type of culture has been added: postmodern culture.

TRADITIONAL CULTURES

Traditional cultures, sometimes referred to as classical cultures, are those that operate as they have for centuries with little change. Religion is at the center of this culture. The authority of the elders, usually also important religious figures, is absolute. Nature is perfect and complete as it is because it was created by God (gods). Order is permanent, while change is incidental. There is a list of moral absolutes, many stated in negative terms. Traditional Christian theology is shaped by classical Greek thought with Scholastic and neo-scholastic categories that are seen as universal. It might be said that keeping the status quo marks this traditional category of culture.

An example of traditional culture can be seen in the conflict between the millennia-old belief in creationism and the then decades-old belief in evolution; this was the subject of a civil lawsuit argued in 1925 during the famous Scopes Monkey Trial in Tennessee. It is a significant example of the tension between traditional and modern cultures, a tension that continues without resolution to this day with creationism now often called "intelligent design."

MODERN CULTURES

Modern cultures are a result of the changes brought about by the Enlightenment and the rise of nation states, together with the ascendancy and use of modern scientific methods despite philosophical, political, and religious objections, as well as divisions that continue to exist. In a modern culture religion is one area of life, nature is always changing, and new discoveries make new demands on society. In modern cultures, process is the norm rather than the exception and it is marked by a move to democracy. The long-running tension between modern views and traditional views has not been totally resolved and to complicate things, the term *postmodern* has evolved and is being widely invoked as a way of explaining what is taking place in the world today.

The modern era began with the deconstruction, or distrust, of accepted interpretations within traditional cultures. Certain interpretations were found to be inadequate. Thus, the modern era developed by providing more or different facts from further experience, resulting in new interpretations. If success in the traditional culture depended on received knowledge (customs, facts, and interpretations of both), success in modern culture depended on knowledge gained from experience or from fresh experience, usually through the scientific method, from the experts. Modern optimists expected that with time and technique all knowledge could be discovered, leading to the secrets of the universe being revealed and conquered. However, knowledge *continues* to unfold and the secrets of the universe *continue* to reveal themselves.

POSTMODERN CULTURES

After more than three centuries down this road of discovery, it has become apparent that with each new thing learned, more unknowns are also discovered. Therefore, a distrust of earlier "new" facts and knowledge emerges. The newest era is no longer modern and it is not yet named beyond being referred to as the postmodern era. There is no reason to believe traditional cultures will not become more modern or even postmodern in their philosophy and behavior. We cannot predict the future; we can only anticipate it with open minds and hearts. Catholic parishes will need trained ministers to help people negotiate emerging points of view. It will require patience, sensitivity, and a true willingness to uncover the deeper truths God continually reveals. This book is designed to help ministers think with a more open mind and recognize the good and the truth in different philosophies and cultures

Not one of the categories—traditional, modern, or postmodern—in and of itself is simple and complete; each category shares characteristics with the others. They are all constructed theories on culture and each one attempts to help in understanding the complex reality of experience. It is difficult to point to a purely traditional or modern culture. The question to consider is, Where are most of the characteristics?

It is important to remember that culture is always in process. Tensions, stresses, and strains are part of the processes that pull or push cultural change. Naturally and humanly created developments also have their effects. Culture can be affected and changed by the personality of those in leadership positions or by the introduction of a new tool or weapon. There are many examples to explain this, but for our purposes we will look at what happens to a parish community when a new pastor arrives. Depending on the personality and management style of the new leader, membership and enthusiasm will flourish or wane. For a time the fall or rise can be attributed merely to change itself; however, over a period of time, it is the way the leader engages the parish community that makes the difference in the community. Paul Wilkes discusses this in depth in his book *Excellent Catholic Parishes* (New York/ Mahwah, NJ: Paulist Press, 2001). Paying attention to the diverse groups in the parish and working to bring them to a point of understanding of the common goal of evangelization, all the while recognizing their differences, define the good leader. His or her training, as well as that which is offered to the parish, will insure a parish culture that embraces each diverse group. It is not as difficult as some may think. The simple sharing of stories, the act of listening to the stories with open minds, and then moving from that point to planning will change parish life.

Any technological, ideological, medical, or sociological change that is incorporated into the existing culture affects the total culture. The introduction of the idea that all people were created equal, the development of the internal combustion engine, and the discovery of bacteria and vaccination all took a significant amount of time to become widely regarded and used within a culture. There are few, however, who would dispute the value they bring to the culture. The introduction of nuclear weapons changed the way nations dealt with each other. The devastation nuclear weapons pose to entire regions of the world leads governments to talk and negotiate rather than resort to using those weapons to settle differences. Likewise, the introduction of the personal computer changed the way the world communicates and does business.

The interests, convictions, and agendas of religious leaders play a big role in how their followers live, both privately and publicly in the community. A religious leader who values dialogue and collaboration or a leader who holds the last word determines how the culture of the parish or even specific committees lives. Dialogue and collaboration usually lead to more creative committees and communities, which reach out to the world in an attempt to make positive change. Communities that are directed primarily on the convictions or wishes of their leader tend to become rigid and inward thinking. However, this too can change as the culture expands and new ideas are brought into the group. Culture moves despite leadership. The members of the culture ultimately make the difference that causes the shift.

As we have stated previously, the human task is to construct meaning and to develop identity. Too often this is seen as a one-time task of growing up and becoming an adult, meaning that when one reaches adulthood, one is complete. However, now we know that nothing could be further from the truth as human beings continue to develop and change throughout their entire lifespan. How else could we explain a sixty-year-old woman pursuing a doctoral degree, or a seventy-five-year-old man deciding to train for a marathon? If upon adulthood we are complete, why would a married man with five children decide at age forty-eight to become a deacon, or why would a priest in the Episcopal tradition for a number of years decide that ordination as a Catholic priest is his calling? Why would a woman, secure and confident in her Catholicism, begin to question the validity of ordination only for males? Humans develop, evolve, and change over time. The culture in which they exist does the same.

This notion of continual change and growth is a beautiful and exciting part of life, yet some see it as threatening and always want to return to "how it was." Fear of the unknown can be stifling to the individual and the institution. When one notices or comes into contact with another culture, there is a natural tendency to revert to the ways of one's culture of origin. While this is natural, it has to be checked to be sure it is not just a discomfort with change but a valid assessment of whatever the situation or circumstance is. No interpretation by an individual or by a culture is immune from questions of legitimacy or reliability and for this we can be thankful. Each culture is the sum total of the inheritance of those things that aid the members of the culture. When a group of people's worldview changes, we say their culture changes so that everyone lives in the new culture that has been created. There is no foreseeable time when all cultures will become one. The task of each culture is to prepare its people to deal honestly with all the new facts that emerge amid new contexts and contacts.

Cultural evolution is a move along the continuum from traditional to postmodern. One of the characteristics of many of today's postmodern cultures is to be more tolerant of diversity. There are many facts and part of life that are understood, but there is also great skepticism of one grand scheme of understanding. There are those who say that in trying to create that grand scheme we either try to take the place of God or we undervalue the mystery of God. However, faith can be expressed in different ways, as seen in "Categories of Culture and Faith," handouts 20a (English) and 20b (Spanish).

Religious conflicts are more understandable if they are seen within the process of the movement of culture along a continuum. A grandmother in the traditional category may insist that the priest, who in her opinion is an expert in life, has the definitive truth about sexual morality, while her granddaughter, in a post-modern fashion may respond, "Whatever," with a bit of a puzzled frown on her face. It may be said that neither of them have the ulti-mate truth but rather their own interpretation of fact, which is what culture is all about.

QUESTIONS FOR DISCUSSION AND REFLECTION

1. Based on the descriptions of the three types of cul-ture—traditional, modern, and postmodern—where do you fit in and why?
2. Are you willing to try to understand someone who identifies with a category of culture that is different from the one you embrace?

FOR FURTHER REFLECTION

"We go about our daily lives understanding almost nothing of the world or culture. We give little thought to the machinery that gen-erates the sunlight that makes life possible, to the glue that glues us onto an earth that would otherwise go spinning off into space. We give equally little thought to why we notice some things and not others, why we accept the roles we play and the way we think." Carl Sagan, "Introduction," in Stephen Hawking, *A Brief History of Time* (New York: Bantam Books, 1988), ix.

6
The Effect of Culture on the Church and Faith

For the LORD *your God...executes justice for the orphan and the widow, and...loves the strangers, providing them with food and clothing. You shall also love the stranger, for you were strangers in the land of Egypt.*
Deuteronomy 10:17–19

Culture affects everything we are and everything we do, including how people relate to the Church and how the Church relates to people. The time has come for the Church to recognize a need for a theology of and a practical blueprint for intercultural understanding that reflects the Christian tradition.

Over the centuries, as travelers, explorers, and missionaries discovered different cultures, the Church faced decisions about how to relate to each of these new cultures. It was not always an easy task or one that can be looked back upon with complete favor. With the discovery of the New World and its inhabitants—the Native Americans in both North and South America—the question was posed whether the newly found groups of people, so different from the Europeans, were really human. Shocking as this seems, it was the harsh reality of the time.

In the context of the globalization of the world today, differing cultural contacts and interactions are quite common. Yet within the Church, tensions still exist, locally and nationally. The Catholic Church, and any other religion for that matter, cannot uproot culture. It must work *with* culture, influencing it and broadening it for the good of the people. A people's natural ability to freely form and develop their culture is one of the greatest gifts they receive from God, an essential part of their personhood. In fact, it is *the* way they become part of their society, as explained in chapter 4. Therefore, the Church ideally strives to follow the "style" of Jesus' mission, proclaiming the good news within a certain culture; yet it also strives to keep in mind that no culture can fully contain the good news of the gospel.

Religions, with rich traditions and ceremonies, are meant by their very nature to celebrate and encourage cultural forms of worship, understanding that every person brings himself and herself and their culture to God, asking for blessings and offering thanksgiving.

If the Church is to become relevant in a particular culture, the gospel and all readings from Scripture have to be proclaimed, either through words or actions, in a way that the particular culture can understand. This can mean a certain language, vernacular, or style. In order to properly proclaim the gospel in a specific culture, that culture must be understood by the person doing the proclaiming. This includes not only its oral and written language, but also its nonverbal methods of communicating. Proclaiming the gospel, often thought of as the role of the priest, is also the role of every minister; therefore, it follows that all ministers need to be aware at all levels of ministry of the culture they are serving.

It is necessary to understand body language, eye contact, and the use of slang words if the Word of God is to be proclaimed and applied to the lives of the people who make up the culture. There is no one quick way to achieve this. It takes time to learn what a culture has to offer and how it operates. This creates a tremendous responsibility for every minister and parish leader, worker or staff, and especially the foreign-born priest or minister coming to the United States to work. Every parish has various cultures and subcultures that have to be honored if the parish is to be effective serving the ministerial needs of its people.

What is the best way to learn together and teach each other? Certainly books, articles, and movies can help describe the American culture, but it will be best accomplished by sharing lives, by inviting the newcomer to the table to eat, drink, and celebrate with us. Over time individuals reveal themselves to each other. The learning is always reciprocal; each participant teaches something of themselves and their culture, and each participant learns.

It is not only the clergy who need to be aware of the importance of learning about cultural differences; all baptized people within the Church also need to learn this. It is the responsibility of the leaders of parish communities to see that this takes place. In some cases that will be the pastor or other clergyman, and in other cases it will be a lay leader. Who takes charge is not important; that it is done is of utmost importance. All people need to be recognized for their God-given gifts and culture.

This is not to imply that the gospel proclamations be changed according to the culture doing the proclaiming. Rather, it is the culture that will understand the gospel according to their practices and traditions. The embodiments of gospel values will inevitably call for changes or conversion in each culture. Culture is an unending work in progress. No culture is absolute (though some may think otherwise). Gospel values are the standards by which Christians scrutinize cultural characteristics.

It is imperative that ministers within the Church pay close attention to the dynamics of the cultures in which they serve. Culture is not static; it changes constantly. A culture that does not understand this becomes sterile, lacking creativity and caring, and it can happen in any parish.

A leader or minister who begins to operate as if his or her culture were the only culture of significance becomes isolated from much of what is actually happening and eventually runs the risk of being ineffective or, as the younger generation would say, "being out of it." We see it happen as once-dynamic parishes fade and people move away to a place that recognizes their needs, which includes celebrating their differences.

The sign of the times cannot be ignored if the Church is to serve as a salt, leaven, and light to the world. The Church, the parish, and everyone involved at every level have to recognize that meeting the needs of the people in the pews where they are the most comfortable is a primary priority for the Church of the twenty-first century. It means putting aside some of our judgments, changing some of our ways of operating, and accepting that the Holy Spirit is at work bringing the world's peoples together. To do less than this will result in a diminished Church, a Church that is ignored and deemed unimportant in the world. This recognition will require members of the Church, both lay and clergy, to listen to each other, learn from each other, and then make decisions made on the information garnered from the discussion. It will require an open mind and heart. For those familiar with theologian Margaret Farley, the above is an example of what she calls "the grace of self-doubt." Margaret Farley, "Ethics, Ecclesiology, and the Grace of Self-Doubt." (See resources available online for full reference [www.paulistpress. com; search *Culture-Sensitive Ministry*].)

It is important to note that the understanding of what is meant by "mission" has undergone a tremendous shift over the past few decades. It has moved from a geographical emphasis to a cultural and theological one. We no longer stress the importance of converting "them," those people far away in foreign lands. Instead we find "them" living among us, which changes the meaning of "mission" and illustrates the priority this understanding of culture has become.

It is our hope that thinking about this shift will motivate you to look at your own parish community and use some of these thoughts to broaden its hearts and minds. In the following chapters we suggest tools that bring people together to appreciate and learn about the cultural differences present in our Church communities and society at large.

The following is a summary list of essential points for reflecting on the complex relationship between faith and culture, especially as it influences pastoral approaches. Any one of them can be used for reflection and for discussion, leading to more understanding and change within the parish community.

1. Discover the cultures of your particular area, seek to unlock their mysteries, learn the intricacies, both general and specific, and remember that at the point you think you understand, realize there is always more to learn, even if it is about your own culture,

because every culture is constantly adapting to its environment and changing.

2. Never forget that Jesus, at a specific time and place in history, became incarnate in a *particular* culture. Modern Scripture scholars are demonstrating the extent to which we came to know God's revelation through these human means.

3. The concept of "culture" is a fairly recent development in the history of thought, one not clearly acknowledged in the Church until Vatican II. Ponder more of what your group says and thinks of this.

4. John Paul II founded the Pontifical Council for Culture in 1983, a significant sign of culture's relevance to the modern world. Read what he had to say when he established this organization and use it as a jumping-off point for introducing cultural awareness to your parish. (See resources available online for full reference at: http://www.paulistpress.com/Culture-Sensitive_ Ministry.html)

5. Pay close attention to the dynamics of culture. They are not static. Do not ignore the signs of the times in both society and the Church.

6. In order to proclaim the gospel in a particular culture, you have to understand the culture, including its oral and written language and its nonverbal ways of communicating. In the style of Jesus, proclaim the good news within a culture, keeping in mind that no culture can fully contain it, as it is *a*-cultural or outside, around, and above any particular culture.

7. Religion should not attempt to uproot culture. It is one of the greatest gifts humankind has received from God and is essential for individuals to become part of their society. The process of presenting the gospel effectively to people of a culture is known as enculturation.

8. It is important to recognize that different manifestations of popular piety or religiosity have been the

way given cultures lived out their Christianity, espe-cially in situations where clergy have been scarce. Be careful not to dismiss this because it seems to you sentimental or simplistic.

9. Cultural dialogue, a way in which a gospel is preached, permits a renewed understanding of the goodness found in each culture. Yet, the embodiment of gospel values will inevitably call for changes, or conversion, in each culture. No culture is absolute. Rather, gospel values are the standard by which Christians scrutinize cultural characteristics.

10. People and cultures develop at the same time. They are influenced from within the Christian community and from outside of it.

11. Intercultural communication is increasingly neces-sary as diverse groups of people migrate throughout the country and across the world. As corporations develop skills to address this phenomenon so should the Church.

12. A theology of intercultural understanding is needed. Seeking unity amid diversity is a Christian tradition since the days of the early Church.

13. Current understanding of "mission" has shifted from a geographical emphasis to a cultural and theological one. We are seeing the need to examine our own Christian communities to see how we are carrying out the mission of the Church.

14. Knowledge is a great aid to help with necessary adjustments in life. Most adjustments are made unconsciously, but many require conscious reflec-tion and decision. A phrase worth remembering is *Change is inevitable, growth is optional.* (The phrase is often attributed to Walt Disney.)

QUESTIONS FOR REFLECTION AND DISCUSSION

Any of the above fourteen points can be used for reflection or discussion.

FOR FURTHER REFLECTION

"We are tempted to suggest that we should be free of institutions. However, there is no such thing as being free of institutions. Humans are incurably institutional and we wouldn't be functional without institutions. It is the institutions that give us the words and the beginnings of a sense of what they mean, if only by frustrating our sense that 'we know it all already' making us undertake long studies in theology during which we may have the fortune to discover that what we thought we knew already was a journey into an unknown and wonderful world." James Alison, *Undergoing God: Dispatches from the Scene of a Break-in* (New York: Continuum, 2006), 92.

PART TWO
The Process

7
Place and Time

He has told you, O mortal, what is good;
and what does the LORD *require of you*
but to do justice, and to love kindness,
and to walk humbly with your God?

Micah 6:8

When planning meetings and gatherings, it is common to concentrate on "the agenda" and to overlook other equally important issues, such as environment, space, time, and process. In this chapter suggestions for desirable locations as well as the use of space and time will be discussed. The following chapters (chapters 8 and 9) will focus on the process.

LOCATION

The best locations to effectively implement the process described in this book are those that are pleasant and quiet and are some distance from the regular work environment of the participants. This says to those participating that the experience is apart from the ordinary, a special time. The goal is to create a period of time for participants to be free from interferences and to focus on the process at hand. If a retreat house is available, it is the preferred venue, as it offers quiet yet ample space for all the interaction necessary to work through the process. However, any facility that offers the same quality of environment is suitable; for instance, a parish hall, an area in a diocesan center, or a school that offers plenty of room to move around and to create small groups for discussion and socializing.

47

INITIAL GATHERING

The gathering time should be clearly stated in the invitation so that when participants arrive for the initial meeting they have plenty of time for registration. If the participants are spending the night, then more time will be needed for selecting rooms, unpacking, and getting themselves "personally ready." During this time the leaders need to greet each individual and encourage introductions and conversation among arriving participants. It is important to remember that at least some of the attendees will be nervous and unsure of themselves. Some will be shy by nature and others may be apprehensive of the unknown process that lies ahead of them. Nametags help people become acquainted. The first meeting of the group should be specific, with food and drink appropriate to the time of day. For instance, if the initial gathering is at 10:00 a.m., it should be followed closely by lunch. If the initial gathering is at 4:00 or 5:00 p.m., then dinner should follow. A major meal is always a good beginning as it provides a relaxing atmosphere and offers generous hospitality to everyone. (See handout #7, "Sample Schedules for Workshops," available online at: http://www.paulistpress.com/Culture-Sensitive_Ministry.html)

USE OF SPACE

For any environment the use of space and the arrangement of chairs are important to the success of the program. Chairs should be comfortable but not plush, as that might encourage slumping or even dozing and it is important that all participants stay alert. Arranging chairs in a circular setup is the most beneficial as it allows space for movement and eye contact among the participants. If the group is large, two concentric circles can be created to keep the space in the middle from becoming too big. There should be plenty of walking space between the circle and the walls of the room so that if people need to move around they feel comfortable. To avoid distraction, movement needs to be around the outside of the group rather than across the middle of the group. It is best to keep people close together with only a small space

48

between chairs. This contributes to creating a community feeling within the group. It also works better to have the circle a bit skewed rather than perfect. There is something about a slightly uneven look that puts people at ease. The slightly informal yet close arrangement focuses and concentrates the energy of the group and adds to the community-building effect. Too much open space encourages individual separation from the group.

It is very informative for the leaders to observe the manner in which participants settle themselves in the space and group. During the group meeting, it is always revealing to watch how each person reacts to the space arrangement. Some will push back to the farthest edge of the circle, while occasionally someone will try to pull a chair completely *outside* the circle. It is important to take note of this as that person may be seeking to be an observer rather than a participant and will remain an "outsider" to the group. Throughout the day, after meals and breaks, it is helpful to reform the chairs in the original circle. It is a subtle way to keep bringing the group together.

Leaders and facilitators sit in the circle at the same level and in the same space as the participants. This enhances bonding and learning as well as subtly communicates that the power within in the group is to be shared. It is a move away from the traditional power position of kings, popes, presidents, and even presiders at liturgies, who sit a bit removed from the group. The program leaders may stand to write on newsprint or a board to make a point in a discussion, but the board is set within the circle or just behind a leader's chair before the group meets so that the movement is natural and logical, again keeping everyone on the same level within the same space.

A large area around the sides of the room is left open as this provides a "backstage" for participants. This extra space around the periphery gives everyone the opportunity to enter the room and the group at their own speed. It provides a place for private space along the integration process. It eases people into the group, which offers comfort and choice rather than direction. It is also a subtle indicator to the group that although everyone is present, they do not all have to speak. It is important to remain conscious, however, that during their time together everyone within the groups must be encouraged to join into the discussions at some time or another.

Some people have to be gently drawn out while others need to be cautioned to listen more and be attentive to what is being said. Every group will naturally divide itself along the line of "listeners" and "speakers." Most people are sensitive enough to know when to join a discussion and when to relinquish the position of focus. However, in every group, there is at least one person who needs help with both listening and speaking. It is up to the leaders to provide gentle direction with this. Every person in the group has to have the opportunity to speak; some need encouragement, others need reining in.

As a focal point for conversation within this backstage, reference books, newspapers, periodicals, or books of 3-D pictures may be displayed. (See resources section online.) The 3-D pictures are used for conversation icebreakers, as well as learning tools about how people view the same things with a different eye. These are used as practical examples of how cultures view each other. The longer and better that one looks at a 3-D picture, the more he or she will see. So it is with culture. We also encourage the reading of newspapers, at least the headlines. This is part of "knowing the signs of the times." Newspapers also develop common language skills and use of idioms. This "backstage space" also invites participants to gather in pairs, small groups, or on their own before the group starts. This gives those from the same culture the opportunity to chat or for new relationships to begin between those of different cultures. These interactions are left to chance; it is not necessary to control them.

Breakout space is needed for small groups to meet for interaction. The location of the breakout space needs to be in close proximity to the group meeting space so time is not wasted moving around and concentration is not lost. Some groups can meet in the same room if it is large enough. The walls of the main meeting room are used to hang newsprint at various times throughout the process. This keeps the process and contents within the view of the participants as the group moves from one topic to another. It triggers thoughts and emotions that otherwise might be overlooked. We recommend not removing newsprint from the walls until the meeting is over.

All of the group functions should take place in the same space with the exception of meals and recreation time. The eucharistic liturgy, however, can be celebrated in either the same room or in a chapel if one is available. This decision can be made on the spot, as it does not have to be predetermined. This is discussed further in chapter 10. The purpose of keeping everything in the same venue is to keep the group together, focused on the task at hand rather than occupied moving things around, which takes energy and time that can be applied to the group process.

The lighting in the room should be varied so full light can be used for discussions, dimmer light for prayers and liturgy, and dark for viewing videos.

USE OF TIME

It is important to maintain the stated schedule. This is a subtle reminder to the group that every participant is important. If the group is waiting past the designated meeting time to begin a session because of stragglers, the leader is penalizing those who have arrived on time. If the group starts without everyone present, those who arrive late find that they miss out rather than that they are so important everyone waited for them; likewise, when someone is late, the group should not stop to review and "catch them up." Each person determines his or her own schedule without penalty but the latecomers do have to play catch up—on their own.

Walking to and from meals is recommended as this is a time when people connect personally. There is also personal time for prayer, exercise, and rest built into each day. Again, see the schedules section. It is important that meals are nutritious, tasty, and presented in an appealing manner. If people are fed well, they tend to progress through the day in a more open state of mind than if they are fretting about dirty tables, shoddily prepared food, or even not enough food. Plenty of nonalcoholic beverage options and snacks should be available throughout the day. Food and drink offer an opportunity for socializing as well as nutrition. In the evening, beer and wine are available as well as nonalcoholic drinks.

Bathroom breaks are left up to the need of the individual, and work breaks are kept to a minimum, as they tend to disrupt the focus and the energy of the group. Our experience indicates that most people can go at least one and one-half hours comfortably without a break, so we use that as our guide. If there are distractions, the content of the discussion is insufficient, or the process is not working, the participants will notice the time and want a break. If all is going well and the discussion is engaging, time is forgotten. After working hard for the entire day, the group is certainly tired but also energized.

Cell phones and pagers should be in the off position unless their use is absolutely necessary. Both of these devices tend to be major distractions to individuals as well as the entire group and contribute to loss of valuable time if they are continually interrupting the flow of conversation and thought.

IN CONCLUSION

Every culture has a personal space "bubble" that allows them to be comfortable. The United States seems to have the largest "bubble" needs, approximately twenty-four inches. Regardless of the space each of us needs, we also need community time and space. A basic skill for effective ministry is the ability to create that community time and space with strangers and others we do not know well. Some people are quicker to make friends, more flexible, or more adaptable. Others are shy and afraid to reach out to others, not knowing what to say or how to initially engage another person. Throughout the program the leaders should model behavior that is inclusive, consistently welcoming everyone, and at times seeking out the quiet or shy people in the group. Sometimes the ease with which a stranger makes friends within the group is indicative of his or her flexibility or willingness to adapt to life and/or ministry in the U.S. culture. The participants' use of space and their adaptation to the group are noted throughout the program. This aids the leadership in their community-building efforts.

QUESTIONS FOR REFLECTION AND DISCUSSION

1. From your experience of group process, what is reinforced by reading this chapter?
2. Does anything in this chapter offer a different perspective?

FOR FURTHER REFLECTION

"We know that all things work together for good for those who love God, who are called according to his purpose." Romans 8:28

8
Pedagogical Methods

"Everyone then who hears these words of mine and acts on them will be like a wise man who built his house on rock."
Matthew 7:24

INTRODUCTION

In this chapter we deal specifically with an overview of the entire pedagogical process. This chapter will lead the reader step by step through the learning process that takes place within the program.

Our program is meant to change the way people relate to each other, and we are pleased to report that in most cases it does just that. Our goal is to broaden one's awareness of the "other" in hopes of expanding the participants' understanding of themselves and others. We use an adult learning model. A large part of the material utilized in the workshops comes directly from the experiences of the participants. Therefore, the primary task is to motivate each person to recall what he or she knows and/or has experienced about the designated topic of the day. We emphasize that students are their own best teachers. We find this facilitates a deeper level of learning. There are no lectures, no note taking, and no exams. This model is designed to be an experience that touches the heart of the participant and brings about some sort of change in his or her manner of thinking and of relating to others.

For example, the first order of business in each session of each workshop is to ask the participants what their experience is with the topic at hand. Everyone who wants to contribute is heard. The knowledge of those participating is the springboard into discussion. Only after this has taken place do we offer "expert" views. It is our experience that participants are quite happy to see that what comes from them is often similar to what comes from the "experts" who contribute through their written words in the handouts.

The learning that takes place in this program is brought about through the experiences shared among the participants. The cultural orientation program supplies words and concepts to help participants understand and relate their varied experiences and reactions in life. It is the experiences (stories) shared among the participants within the cultural orientation program that bring about greater learning.

Because we are aware that people's lives are busy with family, work, and ministry, we recommend that the process be divided into short, intensive sessions within the framework of three workshops, each one conducted over a number of days, usually two or three. We schedule each workshop at least a few months apart. This structuring entails more expense of time and travel but our experience and the feedback from participants indicate that increased learning results from using this type of scheduling. Participants have time in between the workshops to think and live what they have learned, making each subsequent workshop more meaningful.

Participants are encouraged to observe how the material presented in the individual sessions within each of the three workshops applies to their lives and to the work they are doing. They are given homework to complete in between workshops that consists of answering questions based on the application of what they learn in the workshops to their environment. When participants return for each workshop, we spend time reviewing and discussing homework with them. This serves two purposes. First, it reminds them that they are personally responsible for learning and applying what they learn. They hear insights and experiences from other participants about the homework and how it can result in clearer understanding and acceptance of cultural differences and concepts. Second, a discussion of the homework serves as a built-in review of the previous session's learning and materials, thus saving time.

A GENERAL OVERVIEW OF THE PROGRAM

Hospitality

Hospitality is vital to the success of the program. Each workshop, which lasts the equivalent of two days and is divided up into sessions, begins with the meeting and greeting of each participant individually in order to help make them feel welcome and secure. They are then shown to their room in a leisurely manner with housekeeping details explained and are given a schedule of the first activities and meetings. (See "Sample Schedules for Workshops" online at: http://www.paulistpress.com/Culture-Sensitive_Ministry.html)

We are acutely aware that touch is a human essential, an important human experience and form of communication. We are also aware that there are cultural differences that allow or frown on handshakes and hugs or other forms of touch. These differences are honored, to the best of our ability, as people are welcomed into the program.

Hospitality can be misunderstood so it is wise to be aware of the cultural expectations of the people in the group coming to each workshop. A priest in one of the workshops shared an example of this type of misunderstanding. He told of coming to the United States from a foreign country and being met at the airport. He was driven to the rectory, shown a room, and handed a key by the pastor, who told him that he would preside at the 8:00 a.m. Mass the next day. The pastor then informed him that he would be away for two weeks vacation, but said there was a microwave in the kitchen he could use for meals. The pastor handed him a beeper to keep because the hospital might call for a priest. And then the pastor departed. The newly arrived priest was left on his own. He had all the tools: a beeper for the hospital, a schedule of Masses he was expected to preside at, and permission to use the microwave oven. He did not, however, have any hospitality—a natural expectation—extended to him, and he was left feeling cold, strange, and lonely.

The reverse also happens. Fr. Ken was looking forward to a trip to the Philippines. He was hoping to get away for a few days

56

on his own at the end of the trip for some solitary time for rest and relaxation. He explained his desire, but the culture of the hosts overwhelmed his hopes and words. In Philippine culture, it is considered rude to leave a guest alone. He was somewhat frustrated when his hosts kept offering trips to the beach and invitations to dinner that left him with no free time for himself.

When Anne was traveling to Italy with her children and one very young grandchild, she had a similar experience. Thankfully her daughter, sensitive to the Italian culture due to living in Italy for an extended period of time and marrying a man from that region of the world, set the stage for her family so they knew that, upon arriving at their destination, they would be offered an elegant afternoon meal. The family, tired from the long flight and wanting only to be left alone to rest, saved themselves and Anne's daughter from an embarrassing afternoon by putting their jet lag aside and entering into the hospitality of the culture they entered.

These examples, while explained in the context of cultural awareness, are also examples of human kindness and courtesy. To reiterate what was said at the beginning of this chapter, the goal of the workshops is to heighten personal awareness and understanding of self and others. On the most basic human level, this means recognizing the effectiveness of common courtesy.

Food is an important part of hospitality. Therefore, we suggest all workshop sessions begin with a meal or a short gathering session just prior to the workshop that offers ample refreshments. This aids in making people comfortable and helps with group cohesion.

Each participant is given a nametag and asked to write the name they want to be called on the nametag. One may write Mr., Mrs., or Ms. and their last name; another will write Fr. Carl; yet another may simply write Carl; and still others will use nicknames. This exercise helps everyone understand how formal or informal they expect to be treated at the moment. It often happens that later in the program nametags are redone. For leaders who are observant, this exercise reveals part of the person's story.

Handout #1 (for all handouts go to http://www.paulistpress.com /Culture-Sensitive_Ministry.html) offers an overview of the entire process as it might look in an ideal situation. Handout #2 presents the goals and objectives of the program. Handout #7 offers examples of schedules for both trainers (leaders) and participants. Copies of these three handouts are given to the participants during the first session of the first workshop.

Storytelling

Sharing stories and personal experiences is crucial to this process of learning. The beginning of the first workshop on the first evening is spent with each participant sharing stories about his or her life. The optimum-sized group, consisting of ten to twelve people, will be small enough that everyone has the opportunity to speak and share their story. Sometimes, however, the groups are large and have to be divided into smaller groups. This is done because sharing stories is crucial for the success of the program, and in a big group sharing would be rushed or would not happen at all. This session typically lasts about one and one-half hours with each person given seven to ten minutes to tell the group a bit about their life. This demonstrates the value of each and every group member.

The importance of sharing personal stories cannot be emphasized enough. Personal stories reveal much about the cultural experiences and expressions of a person, as well as how they view God and the world. As program leaders, we try to keep the stories flowing by giving participants freedom to go in any direction they choose. There is never an attempt to bias, question, or focus the story in any particular direction beyond keeping the story progressing. Each person is allowed to deal with ambiguity and the group as they wish. This is to model the idea that each life, each person, is unique and worthwhile. If a person is very brief, we will try to suggest other areas to talk about by asking questions like: What about family, schooling, travel, and so on?

An intended benefit of the storytelling is to alert the participants to the importance of listening. We sometimes ask the group what they heard as a story was told or ask one person from each of the small groups (if a large group has been divided) to introduce another person back into the larger group. This is done not only by using their name but also by telling a very short part of their story, just one or two pertinent facts that give a sense of who the person is. Accurate listening is difficult due to thoughts that the speaker may trigger in the listener's head. However, not listening closely may cause clues of God's Word to be missed. We are convinced that one of the greatest blocks to conversation is inadequate listening.

To begin the first session of the first workshop by telling personal stories is an efficient way to facilitate the introduction of several people at one time. However, on a much deeper level, there is something taking place in the storytelling itself that needs to be appreciated and encouraged. God speaks to each person not only through Scripture and through Church teaching but also through personal experience. This is sometimes forgotten, and in these workshops an attempt is made to get participants to focus on personal experiences, both their own and others', as a way of interpreting life and hearing what God might be trying to say.

The use of personal stories and experiences helps make greater contact between thoughts and emotions. Storytelling reveals thoughts and evokes emotions. Thus, participants are given the opportunity to gain a fuller, deeper appreciation of themselves and others. Paying attention to one's life experience and story is an important step in listening to the prompting of the Spirit, growing in faith, and developing effective ministerial skills. It is a way of dealing with the past, understanding that the strategies used in the past were possibly ineffective, and becoming aware of a new way of living as well as a new way of doing ministry.

Through the group process of storytelling, individuals in the group tend to come together in support of each other. Though tentative at first, through time and effort a trust emerges. The support provides personal affirmation, instills self-worth, and encourages respect for every participant. Furthermore, the events of the group become part of future personal stories.

It is common for the first one or two stories to be rather short and to the point: "This is who I am and this is what I do." As time goes by and others in the group speak up, the stories get longer and longer. A crucial function of the group leader or director is to keep a balance within the group by encouraging the short stories to continue or broaden, as well as to gently guide those who speak too long to abridge their stories. It is common that every group has one or two participants that, if given the opportunity, will speak too much. The skill of keeping the balance takes practice so that it is done kindly and diplomatically.

Group members are encouraged to question the storyteller for information, not explanation, as asking for an explanation may be construed as making a judgment. The shared storytelling by each participant is selective. The group listening may aid the storyteller in more fully integrating various parts of his or her story for clarity. Subsequent workshops will continue to refer back to and build on these stories from the first session.

In our experience with foreign priests, we have repeatedly watched groups of individual priests gather for the first night of the Cultural Orientation Program for International Ministers (COPIM), smiling politely but rather tentatively, unsure of what is to come and therefore being somewhat guarded. A few days later this same group of priests has evolved into a warm, caring community. Often friendships and contacts continue long after the COPIM experience. Similar experiences will occur among parishioners that will build community within the parish long after the program is over. Human behavior is predictable, and lessons learned from one experience, as with the foreign-born priests who have journeyed through this program, are directly applicable to lay groups within a parish.

Methods

At the beginning of this chapter we said that we do not use prepared lectures. Instead, the presenter or leader of each session will spend about five to six minutes giving whatever outline of a topic is necessary before continuing with questions, which each person can answer by drawing from their own experiences. Thus, the personal stories about experiences come into play once again and are more fully developed and shared.

Utilizing the skills of two coleaders for each group of participants has been, in our experience, the best plan for success with these groups. This allows each leader to add points of clarification, ask questions, or offer their own personal experience, while the other leader is guiding the group through a discussion. Done correctly, it is not viewed as interruption but teamwork.

Throughout the workshops, the leaders model sharing, developing further their own personal stories and/or referring to the personal stories or points of view already expressed. In telling their stories leaders should touch on four areas: place of origin, family, education, and work or ministry. This technique assures and models for the group that leadership listens. Thus the leaders become part of the group rather than merely leading the group. A team approach is always most productive as it presents a comfortable atmosphere of shared ownership of the process. This is one of the major learning points throughout the series of workshops.

Two people working as a team give the participants two different personalities and points of view. This team approach creates a relaxed environment whereby group members feel more comfortable contributing. This method gives every person an opportunity to experience an informal, comfortable learning atmosphere as they venture into new areas of ministry or join new groups in a parish.

Leaders are present at all workshops and all sessions even when there are guest speakers. This presence allows the leaders to remain members of the group, avoiding any suggestion of "us and them." When leaders remain present to hear the actual words of the speaker, it aids in discussions and pinpoints areas for the leaders to integrate into the group process.

Leaders do all of the presentations at the first workshop and on the first evening of the other two successive ones. Guest speakers and a panel conduct the presentations during the second and third workshops. The presentations are short and meant to offer diverse opinions and styles of ministry. Following the presentations, participants question the speakers for clarification or information. The large group then breaks up into small groups for discussion of the topic for fifteen or twenty minutes. Each small group agrees on two or three questions to bring back to the larger group for a general discussion of the topic. Participants often use their own experiences to form these questions and reactions. Getting comfortable with diversity and different points of view is the goal of these presentations.

Shared male/female responsibility in ministry is an issue that must be addressed. Women offer insight on women's theological concerns and perspectives and explain their positions of power and influence within dioceses and parishes. Speakers are also included who present their views and experiences on ethnic issues, addictions awareness, liturgical guidelines, and modes of operation. The workshops have been developed to create a welcome, safe space where feelings, questions, and even hurts can be dealt with in a respectful manner.

GENERAL OVERVIEW OF SESSIONS WITHIN THE THREE WORKSHOPS

Each individual session within each workshop has a theme or focus and is opened with a short presentation—a sort of introduction that sets the tone for the session. This is followed by either large or small group interaction. It is imperative that every person be able to listen to another's comments and questions regarding the topic presented. It is also important that each person be able to articulate what they have heard, make comments, and voice questions. To facilitate this interaction the large group can be divided into smaller groups of four or five and given fifteen to twenty minutes to talk among themselves on the topic presented. An alternative to this is to have two participants talk together without leaving the large group. If this interaction is chosen, the time limit is five to seven minutes.

Large pieces of newsprint are given to each group so they can record the points they believe are salient. These pieces of newsprint are hung on the wall where the large group meets and all participants are given time to read the comments before the large group reconvenes for group discussion. We do not have group reports as they tend to get very boring. Any person may ask any group what they meant by a word or a phrase on their newsprint.

After this discussion period, the large group is reassembled and participants are asked to share their insights. This gives the entire group an opportunity to hear many different viewpoints and discuss them further.

At this point, the leaders can ask questions or emphasize something about the topic that is deemed important. From the discussion we can gauge what learning is taking place and we continually refer back to our focus points to be sure we have covered everything planned.

We use this process without explaining the process during the workshops. The participants learn at their own speed and from their own perspective. They learn from each other, not just from the leaders and the special presenters. The question "What have you learned?" is repeated a number of times during each workshop to help keep participants focused on their work of learning the purpose of the program.

Being intensely aware, listening, recalling, and discussing are often more taxing than expected, especially for those who do not use English as a first language. We are careful to avoid overload by providing an extended time after lunch for personal use: siesta, walking, reading, exercising, or whatever relaxes or renews the person. The overload can be from material presented as well as from getting used to the new surroundings, people, and the process the program uses. While learning the program's process skills is rewarding in itself, it also provides training for future ministry.

The methodology of this chapter outlined the program's general process skills. In the next chapter we look at the purpose and process for each individual workshop.

QUESTIONS FOR REFLECTION AND DISCUSSION

1. What further reasons for prioritizing skills might be important (that is, listening, paying attention)?
2. From your experience, what happens when each person is allowed to tell her or his own story?

FOR FURTHER REFLECTION

"The stories we tell, whether human or divine, mythic or parabolic, order experience, construct meaning, and build community." Herbert Anderson and Edward Foley, *Mighty Stories, Dangerous Rituals* (San Francisco: Jossey-Bass, 1998), 32.

9
Individual Workshops

Let the wise also hear and gain in learning,
and the discerning acquire skill.

Proverbs 1:5

In this chapter, we deal specifically with the content and process for each workshop and the sessions within each workshop. Each workshop takes place over three consecutive days. Please note that the various handouts suggested to be used are available as online resources. (http://www.paulistpress.com/Culture-Sensitive_Ministry.html)

WORKSHOP #1.
CULTURE AND CULTURE-CROSSING

The *first workshop* begins by concentrating on welcoming: making the participants comfortable and affirming the gifts and skills they bring to the workshop, to their own pastoral ministry, and to the Church. Its overall topic focuses learning on culture and cultural crossing. Time is spent explaining culture, what it is, what it does, and what happens when one crosses from one culture to another culture.

The first evening is spent telling personal stories, as described in chapter 8. The first morning session (day 1) after breakfast and prayer asks the question: What is culture?

Participants are divided into small groups and each group is given two pieces of newsprint. Everyone in the group is asked to think, to share something about their culture, and then to come up with a broad view and definition of culture. Components of culture are written on one newsprint and definition of culture on another.

These newsprints will be brought back to the large group and hung on the walls of the room when participants reconvene into the large group.

A general discussion of culture and of the statements written on the newsprints follows. Everyone is encouraged to ask for clarification or to answer what was meant by a word or phrase if there is something that needs clarification about one of the statements on any of the newsprints. The leaders can help draw out comparisons, variations, and similarities on the newsprint statements.

At the conclusion of this discussion, handouts #3, #4, and #5 (in both English and Spanish versions where appropriate) are distributed. Comments and discussion follow on the representations of culture presented with the handouts. Discussion focuses on both what is positive or believed to be true and what appears to be misrepresented. Handout #3, "Man with Telescope," is a representation of how culture was illustrated at one time. Participants are asked, in the light of the previous discussions, what flaws they can see in the illustration. We direct the discussion to the idea that culture is not something that is outside of each of us, but rather something within each person; also that culture is the lens through which we view the world.

Handout #4a, the "Iceberg," (and 4b, the Spanish translation) depicts the enormous reservoir of culture that exists, illustrating that culture is both conscious and unconscious, probably as much as 90 percent unconscious, signified by having only the tip of the iceberg showing above the water line. We offer that cultural conflicts arise when the unconscious is ignored or perhaps unknown. We refer to what the participants have written on their pieces of newsprint as practical examples of how much they did not think or were not aware of when describing culture, also pointing up the things they did include. Almost universally the topic of technology and its effects on culture are ignored by groups so we initiate a discussion on the enormous effects technology has on culture.

Handout #5a, "Definitions of Culture,"(and 4b) shows that no one definition of culture seems to be adequate. This illustrates that culture is complex, not easily definable.

We give an explanation about the usefulness of stereotypes, their importance, and also the hindrances (the pluses and minuses) that they can bring to an understanding of culture. We also help the participants understand culture, subculture, and a variety of worldviews in this first session together.

The next handout for this session is #6a, "Broad Categories of Culture" (also 6b in Spanish), which explains the differences between traditional, modern, and postmodern cultures. We note that anthropologists classify cultures by similarities and differences. The purpose of handout #6 is to demonstrate that all three of the classifications reveal some things and ignore others. It is difficult to find a culture that fits exactly or exclusively into one category. Remember that creating categories is an attempt to understand and compare complex realities. While most cultures fall predominantly into one category, in reality, some include characteristics from all three. This is an important attempt to show the complexity of culture and how the categories influence different groups within the Church. The aim is to alert participants to be patient, to really listen to people, and to be able to see that all of the categories have positive elements that deserve respect.

Just before the lunch break, participants are given handouts #8a and 8b, "Cross-Cultural Education and Training." We ask them to spend a few minutes before coming together in the afternoon to look over the article, paying particular attention to the progressive categories of learning about culture "entering."

Upon returning from lunch at about 2:30 p.m., we briefly review the morning's take on culture and ask for questions concerning handout #8. This handout, which explains the views of two authors on cross-cultural learning, is purposely included to demonstrate that there is more than one way of looking at the topic. We make clear that, when it comes to crossing a cultural border, it is common in nearly all cases that individuals will proceed according to the knowledge they have of the culture they are entering. Each person moves from fear of the unfamiliar to acceptance. It takes a great deal of time to get to the level of acceptance, and it is rare that anyone completes the process to total integration with, or adaptation to, another culture.

We ask each person to talk to another about how they see themselves moving along the stages toward acceptance; we then move the discussion to the large group. We make it very clear that there is not one stage that is better than another; rather it is a journey that everyone makes at their own pace.

The afternoon session continues with a focus on the characteristics of Americans. This discussion is another major focus of this workshop, the culture of the United States. Again, we begin by asking people to go to their small groups and on newsprint write several characteristics of "Americans" and return the newsprint to the walls of the main room when they are finished. We allot about twenty minutes for the small group discussion.

After each person has read the newsprints we begin a general discussion and try to group and compare the proposed characteristics. It is usual that there are positive and negatively stated characteristics. Handouts #9a and b, "Outstanding Characteristics of Americans," is passed out and discussed in light of what has already been said. We mention that various authors note different characteristics. We choose five different characteristics from handout #9 and look at the positive and negative aspects of each. We also note that some of the newsprints have similar comments on the characteristics of Americans.

This concludes the afternoon session. Everyone takes a short break before Eucharist and dinner.

After dinner we reconvene and ask the participants to recall the entire day. "What did you learn?" is asked a number of times. Every participant is asked to share something they have learned with the large group. It is best if the lighting can be dimmed, setting more of a meditative and reflective tone. This evening session serves as a meditative summary of the day. It is deliberately held after dark with just the participants and the two leaders. We have learned that people speak more freely at night. Emotions emerge, not just intellectual sharing. Darkness outside and dim lights inside pull the group closer together. This is a unique time where anguish can be expressed, learning can be digested, and conversion can take place. We consider this the most important session offered. There is no discussion, just the sharing of learning. As leaders we retain the option of asking questions if we think an important point of the day has been omitted, and we share our own learning.

The goal of workshop #1 is to help each participant remember his or her own cultural history and its importance for their personal values and heritage. This is imperative in understanding cultural development, its variety, and the participant's current experience of differing cultures.

The evening ends with a movie that portrays cultural changes and attendant problems. Movies provide further impetus for thoughts and discussions about race, prejudice, culture-crossing, and culture blindness. We highly recommend the film *Whale Rider* for this first evening. The next morning there is a short discussion of what was seen and/or heard in the movie. An annotated list of suggested movies useful to this process can be found in the online resources.

The morning of day 2 begins after breakfast and prayer with a discussion of cultural learning from the movie shown the previous night. Then we distribute handout #10, "Summary of U.S. Catholic History," taken from *American Catholicism* by John Tracy Ellis (1969). Current culture always grows out of past culture so we try to highlight some important points in United States history. Besides handout #10 on U.S. Catholic history, we use handout #11 on local Catholic history; in our case the *"Historia de la Iglesia en California."* We recommend a short history of the local diocese or state be used here. We sometimes substitute a short section of the documentary, *The Faithful Revolution: Vatican II.* (See online resources.) Either this or the Ellis handout prompt questions, comments, and discussion that lead participants to look at their experience of U.S. culture.

The rest of the morning is spent talking about the effects of culture in bible and theological writing and reading. By 11:30 a.m., we bring discussion to a close and hand out an evaluation form. (See the evaluation section.) As the participants write comments on this evaluation form, they can also make public comments. This helps to remind others of things they may have forgotten or overlooked.

The dates for the next two workshops are given to the participants, as well as homework questions for them to work on in the interim. The questions we use are:

1. *What cultures and subcultures are operating in your place of ministry?*
2. *What do the cultures look like and how do these cultures work?*

WORKSHOP #2.
DIVERSITY OF CULTURE

The *second workshop*, usually held two months or so after the first, again begins with welcoming and affirming the participants; this continues to be a subtle learning tool for how things should, under ideal conditions, take place in culture and Church. This workshop continues community-building and sharing of experiences of work, holy days, holidays, and family.

The topic for this workshop is the diversity of culture, with particular attention paid to tensions in the U.S. culture: male/female relationships, racism, leadership styles, economic class, ethnic issues, gay/lesbian issues, and organizational styles, among other things. These issues are thought to be the ones most needed to help the participants in their daily religious and ministerial lives. A development of healthy relationships within families as well as within the parish, especially with those with whom they might not agree or might see as different, is essential.

The first evening is spent reviewing what was learned in the previous workshop, using the participant's homework.

From our experience, we have concluded that the topics of women as equals, Church teachings about homosexuality, and ethnic conflict have been most important. During the morning session on day 1 of this workshop, we bring in three panelists to make presentations, ten to twelve minutes in length, for each of the topics. When the presentations are complete, participants are given time to digest, discuss, comment, and ask questions of the panelists. This entire presentation is usually limited to forty-five minutes. The panel members are chosen carefully for their knowledge and expertise, as well as for their position in the Church hierarchical authority. Their ability to understand and be part of the group process also determines who is invited to speak. For example, we look for women who hold positions of power in the diocese: chancellor, department head, and so on. Our purpose is to challenge the participants, as well as introduce them to the style of ministry that is followed in the area of the United States where they will reside and practice any ministry.

After the panelists have spoken and the clarifying questions answered, participants gather in small groups for further discussion. Small groups get everyone involved in talking and listening. Each group is given newsprint and asked to agree on and prioritize questions for the presenters. After about twenty minutes the groups reconvene and post their newsprints on the wall. We encourage people to take a ten minute break, as well as read all the newsprints.

By 10:30 a.m., we reconvene for a large group discussion. Each group in order asks a question. The presenter asked will answer the question and the other two presenters may make a comment. The questions range from theological issues to practical issues.

Other sessions concerning liturgy, addictions, and leadership styles are offered throughout the workshop. It should be noted that the topics of addictions—primarily drugs, alcohol, and computer pornography—are a danger especially to those who find themselves isolated, lonely, or overworked. We recognize the need to incorporate awareness of these pitfalls for ministers into the program.

Again we ask speakers to come for presentations on the chosen topic, following the same format: a short presentation, clarifications, and discussions.

There may also be the need to talk about racism. If this is the case we ask the participants to form groups and talk about a time they felt discriminated against. We offer that their experience of discrimination may have been due to the color of their skin, their age, gender, or any number of other things that may come up. When everyone returns to the large group, we make a list by asking each group to mention one thing they discussed about discrimination. We continue, asking each group for other items until the list becomes quite extensive. Handouts #12a and b, "Dismantling Racism," is distributed, followed by a discussion of prejudice and power.

The above topics are chosen specifically for foreign-born priests and nuns; however, the topics are also applicable for lay parish groups. Other pertinent and timely topics can be added for these types of parish groups. The crucial point is that the "experts" brought in to present their ideas be effective and interesting in both their presentations and responses to the questions of the groups.

Liturgy and dinner follow this afternoon session of various topics, and the evening ends with a general session reviewing what was learned during the day.

Please note that at any time in this program, in any session, the process is more important than the content. Therefore, if the discussion is lively and energetic, let it go a bit longer. If the discussion drags, bring it gently to a close.

We begin the evening session by asking once again, "What have you learned today?" The group waits in respectful silence until someone speaks. Everyone is reflecting on what they have experienced and learned during the day, and a comment by another person will spark further thoughts and reflection. This process continues for about an hour and a half, allowing time for everyone to speak, therefore deepening and enriching the reflections of each person. Personal conversion stories or a broadening of one's horizons are shared, often around the issues of homosexuality and women; for example, the realization that women are competent and, in fact. hold leadership positions, and that homosexuals are officially accepted and welcomed in the Church. Insights on how family history has affected one's development or career path or marriage are common as well. There are many "aha moments" during the evening sessions. Every group will come up with their own areas of learning. The learning depends entirely on the topics presented and on the makeup of the group. For example, a group of all women will have a different perspective than a group of all priests or a group of all married people. A group made up of parish staff will have different concerns and experiences than a group of parishioners who are employed outside the structure of the parish. Leaders learn this and are able to guide groups with diverse life experiences through meaningful discussion.

Again, the evening ends with a movie about culture changing or crossing. (See the annotated list of suggested movies in the online resources.)

The next morning's session, day 2, begins with discussion of the movie from the previous evening. This second discussion of a movie always proves to be more spirited and lively than that of the first workshop. When this discussion is complete, the rest of the morning is devoted to the topics of change, fear, and grief. This session is included to remind people that any time change occurs, fear often accompanies it. Participants are asked to move into small discussion groups and compile a list of five to seven things they were sad about the last time they experienced a major change in their lives, such as a move, a job change, or a shift in status. They are also asked to compile a list of fears they felt as they faced these same things. These responses are recorded on newsprint as in previous sessions.

After about fifteen minutes or so, participants post their newsprints on the wall and a general discussion takes place about what is on the newsprints. The discussion reveals similarities between the lists of sadness and the lists of fears. The participants are asked to think about what happens to these feelings. Are they forgotten, buried, or dealt in a healthy manner?

At this point we pass out handouts #13a and b, "Change, Fear, and Grief," and explain that psychologists have extended the grief process. It now includes any type of loss, not just the loss felt at the time of a death of a loved one or significant person in one's life. We explain the grief process as an ongoing process, a circular process, not linear, as many believe, moving from one point to another. The discussion is often lively and exciting as participants discover this new understanding of grief and how it explains feelings that have caused confusion for them.

This session has emerged over the years as an important one. It reminds people that any time a change occurs, fear accompanies it and questions arise. We stress that even positive change brings with it a sense of loss for what was. Sometimes there is an almost audible sigh of relief as participants understand their feelings for the first time in years.

We use concrete examples to explain this phenomenon. After the joyful celebration of a wedding, the parents of the bride or groom realize their child is now different, and there is a bittersweet feeling of loss: their child has moved on to a new life. The same can be said when a young girl goes through her *quinceañera*, a coming-of-age ceremony held on a Hispanic girl's fifteenth birthday. The celebration is wonderful but after the party is over, the parents understand their little girl is grown up. With this comes joy but also new fears. When a son or daughter moves from home to college, he or she experiences similar things. Mom is no longer there to do the laundry, clean the room, or cook the meals. The euphoria of independence gives way to the feeling of loss. Every group will come up with similar but different examples of loss, depending on the makeup of the group. It is important to spend enough time on this topic as it is sometimes seen as weak to feel the pain of the loss. This myth needs to be dispelled.

Before ending the final session of this second workshop, the participants are given homework questions. Participants are asked to go back to the groups and subgroups discovered and reported on before. This time they are asked to research further three questions:

1. *How do groups within your parish view God and theology?*
2. *How is leadership developed and handled in your parish or community?*
3. *How do groups in your parish or community think about and handle diversity?*

WORKSHOP #3.
THEOLOGICAL PERSPECTIVES
AND COLLABORATION

The *third workshop*, which takes place a couple of months after the second, again opens with the affirming, welcoming, and Christian community-building that were put into practice since the previous workshops. The homework questions, distributed at the conclusion of the second workshop, are discussed in small groups and then back in the large groups, as in the prior workshop. At this point a positive sense of camaraderie has developed within the group, due to the fact that participants have been together for two previous extended periods of time and have relaxed into sharing their ideas, opinions, and experiences honestly and openly. The process that has been in place in the previous workshops continues. Participants know what to expect as far as the process goes and are able to move easily through the material. Their inhibitions have been diminished and they are quite comfortable.

After sharing responses to the homework questions on the first evening, the morning session begins with the topic of changing how we think about theology. Handout #14, "Contextual Theology," and handout #15, "Thinking Theologically," are given out.

The first focus is on theological thinking, or "doing theology." We explain that everyone thinks about faith, God, and things of this nature from their own cultural perspective and experience. Since participants have already reflected on their own theological formation and ongoing learning, we ask them to return to their small group and discuss their reflections from this new perspective. On newsprint they record favorite theological topics, as well as theological/spiritual books they have read recently. They are also asked to agree on a definition of what it means to "do" theology.

After fifteen to twenty minutes, everyone returns to the large group and reads the responses posted on the wall in the same method as previous workshops. A discussion on what it means to "do" theology follows. Often participants begin to realize that, while they have understood theology as a body of knowledge to be studied, it is actually an ongoing experience or process lived out in their various ministries throughout the parish community and the community at-large. Thus "doing" theology becomes an awareness of what "I" and others are thinking because of our experiences in light of Scripture and Tradition. This reflection is about what God's Spirit is revealing (saying) now. This learning always generates energy and excitement. The shift to seeing theology as alive and interactive with the community rather than a system of thought is inspiring and motivating for many participants.

The afternoon looks at trends in theology. A major trend—and one of enormous importance to cross-cultural ministry—is contextual theology. This is theology that arises from a particular situation, or context, or from a particular population. Examples are liberation theology, which arises from unjust political or economic conditions; ecotheology, which is a reaction against the misunderstanding and misuse of the idea of stewardship; and so on. This session is followed by a presentation on feminist theology, an often-misunderstood concept.

After a twenty- to thirty-minute presentation by a feminist theologian, there is a question and answer period with the presenter. Following this, participants are asked to move into small groups to discuss what they heard. Each group works for about twenty minutes coming to agreement and prioritizing three or four questions to bring back to the larger group for discussion with the presenter. The questions are written on newsprint as in all the other sessions. When the small groups are finished with their discussion and the large group is reconvened, the presenter replies to the questions from the newsprint posted on the walls, answers any further questions, and adds comments she deems appropriate. It is usual that each small group will ask at least two of the questions they developed, which is the reason they are directed to prioritize the questions. There is never enough time to address every question.

At this point we pass out another copy of handouts #20a and b, mentioned in chapter 5. This looks at the different cultural categories from a theological perspective. Each cultural category will use different kinds of language to express theological issues. This is important for personal perspectives and also especially for ministry. This handout presents different ways of looking at theological matter. These categories have practical use for teaching and catechesis. It helps identify various ways of speaking about God and faith.

The final portion of the afternoon looks at the organization of parishes using handout #16, "Functions of a Parish." The discussion addresses ministry on a concrete and practical level and offers ideas on how to effectively use the talents of everyone in the life of the Church. This part of the afternoon is meant to plant seeds for discussion of collaboration and consensus the next morning.

There is a short break before Mass at 5:15 followed by dinner. We recommend using the movie *Inherit the Wind* for this evening session as it sums up much of what we have tried to pass along to the participants. The movie portrays how religion can be used for good or evil in the heat of political struggles. Although the movie is about the Scopes Monkey Trial that took place in 1925 in Tennessee, it remains relevant today as society grapples with the theories of evolution and intelligent design. It also shows the importance of careful and effective communication among differing points of view.

The final session of this workshop, held in the morning after breakfast and prayers, begins with a discussion of the movie *Inherit the Wind* viewed by the group the previous night. Following this discussion handout #17, "Collaboration," and handout #18, "Consensus," are passed out. It is pointed out to the group that they have heard these words a number of times in this workshop, specifically from the feminist theologian and in the discussion of the functions of a parish. A short discussion is initiated on the importance of the concepts in light of what was said about the functions of a parish the day before using the handouts as examples. Some time is spent on the importance of each ministry or the entire parish developing a workable understanding of the words *collegiality, consensus, collaboration*, and *cooperation*. How does collaboration differ from cooperation? How can a parish or specific ministry arrive at a win–win decision? These types of questions, based on concepts in the handouts, suggest possibilities and motivate participants to return to their ministries and parishes with a set of skills to work more effectively.

As the above schedule indicates, we sometimes shift the use of the handouts, not always using them in chronological order. It is important that each point be discussed, but the order of the discussion can be reversed to allow the free flow of ideas, thus using handouts a bit differently.

Culture-Sensitive Ministry

The final session of the workshop lasts about thirty to forty-five minutes. It is an exercise involving the sharing of graces and is meant to help the group hear and feel God's providence that has engaged them along the way in the learning, the faith-sharing, and the struggling needed for intercultural living.

The exercise is like good spiritual direction. It helps the group members see prayer as becoming aware of how God has been active in their lives, trying to save each of them from things that would rob them of a "life lived to the fullness" as opposed to prayer being a way to "get God to do something about the miserable state I'm in."

There are three questions for this closing discussion. They usually take about thirty to forty-five minutes to discuss:

1. For me, what were the main graces, or gift, of the entire program?
2. What might God be trying to tell me?
3. How might I cooperate with these graces that God is granting me?

The leaders set the tone for this individual sharing held within the circle. They ask for contemplative silence before the sharing begins and then end the sharing with a closing prayer.

One of the most moving aspects of the sharing of graces is that group members often realize that both their companions in the workshops, as well as the communities in which they live, have been an extraordinary grace for them, much the same way that the Lord has accompanied them on the difficult but adventuresome journey of faith.

By about 11:30 a.m., it is again time to bring the workshop to a close, and we give out handout #19, "References for Staying Current on Theological Issues." We also pass out an evaluation form (handout #21—"Sample Evaluations") for the entire program. The participants are asked to fill out the form and are encouraged to speak out loud about any important point they want the entire group to hear.

Following this, name tags and evaluations are placed in the middle of the circle, and everyone steps outside for a small glass of wine to toast the conclusion of the program. Good-byes are said and lunch is available before everyone leaves.

QUESTIONS FOR REFLECTION AND DISCUSSION

1. What aspects of process in this chapter might be most useful for you in a leadership role?
2. In workshops you have attended, what energized you most?
3. Are you aware of God's grace in your life, and if so, does that grace move you to action?

FOR FURTHER REFLECTION

"Process is more important than content." Fr. Ken McGuire, CSP

10

Conclusions
GROWING EDGES AND CONCERNS

The LORD opens the eyes of the blind.
The LORD lifts up those who are bowed down;
  the LORD loves the righteous.
The LORD watches over the strangers;
  he upholds the orphan and the widow.
                              Psalm 146:8–9

We are all part of a learning and growing Church. It is important to keep this in mind as you adapt this culture-sensitive program to your situation. As more immigrants, both lay and clergy, move to the United States, the challenge of integrating them into the parish community increases. Parish staff and leadership have a responsibility to both the immigrant and the established parishioner, and it takes patience and prayer to bring them together. This book is our effort to ease that challenge and shift the phenomenon from burden to opportunity.

The only reason we have been able to write this book is because we ourselves have had good teachers. By generously entrusting us with their life stories and struggles, the participants and presenters have shown us that God's grace is always at work, particularly in circumstances of suffering. Stories shared in the evening hours about early family hurts and concerns, anger, frustration, racism, and misunderstandings—as well as violence in the participants' countries of origin—are poignant and offer a thoughtful perspective for everyone involved.

After coming to the United States and establishing themselves, many of the participants quickly befriend racial minorities and the poor and empathize with their mistreatment or their marginalization by the Church or society in general. As we listen to their stories, we are reminded that the poor and those who suffer have great power to evangelize those of us who might have become complacent about our "well-earned" social status. What we learn by these stories often outweighs what we set out to teach.

Taking some of our own advice about the complexity of cultures, we remain convinced that there is still much more to learn. In fact, the wisest course of action is to continue to experiment with open hearts, minds, and ears; paying attention to the signs of the times, listening carefully, and stretching conventional wisdom.

We remain painfully aware that there are various ways to accomplish the goals we have laid out in this book, each of which has positive as well as negative aspects and results. Therefore, in the sections following, we present three areas that are still problematic, areas where feelings have been hurt or misunderstandings have resulted. For now let us call these three areas the "3 Ls": language, liturgy, and leadership.

LANGUAGE

An issue that arises consistently is that of foreign priests and ministers being understood. Foreign priests are often told that their accents prevent congregations from understanding what they are saying in the prayers of the liturgy and in homilies. The same can be said for any lay minister with a pronounced accent who is proclaiming the Word, making announcements, or teaching in the parish. As can be expected, there are hurt feelings over this and the result is that priests and ministers feel rejected, and parishioners feel frustrated. This program offers a forum for discussing these hurt feelings and frustrations through caring and patient listening to the stories that are shared. It is then up to the parish leaders to address the issue in a way that models compassion and concern for everyone involved.

We suggest that issues of language be addressed in a homily so that all parishioners can be more aware of *their* personal need to work at listening and participating in the liturgy. We also recommend accent-reduction instruction rather than more English classes.

During the program itself, all teaching is done in English. Handouts, however, are translated. Sometimes, if there are several Spanish speakers in the group who do not understand English, professional translators or one of the team will translate simultaneously, sitting next to this group and speaking in a very low voice as not to disturb the others. We encourage English, pointing out that this is a safe environment for making mistakes and learning.

LITURGY

Where to celebrate the liturgy during the program—in a chapel or in the same room as the workshop—is a legitimate question. However, it does not have a definitive answer. The chapel signals a more formal setting, a traditional way, and a time set apart to worship together. Celebrating the liturgy in the same room where the workshop is held is informal and reinforces the idea that worship is one of many activities for priest and people. This choice is reminiscent of gatherings of early Christian communities.

Whatever the choice, the liturgy should be simple with an eye to including the needs and prayers of the participants, with special notice taken for their participation in the workshops. It is logical that the diversity of cultures represented be honored.

For the first several years we offered a section on racism: "Dismantling Racism," handout #12. However, the feedback from bishops, pastors, and laypeople suggested the need for more time spent on American liturgical practices, especially cooperation of liturgy planning teams, musicians, presiders, and preachers, as well as the various liturgical possibilities in the guidelines. Since there is limited time, we dropped racism and substituted liturgy. Both are important and it is up to the local leaders to decide what to include or omit. The decision on what to discuss depends on the climate in the parish or community at the time the workshops are offered, as well as the overall climate of the Church and society in general. The participants, guided by the Spirit, will take the discussions where they need to go for the most benefit for all. The wise leader will allow for turns in the road.

LEADERSHIP STYLES

In every group there are a variety of cultures represented and therefore many differing expectations. There is no way to meet all expectations. Culture crossing can be delightful, illuminating, and challenging. Yet it can also be dangerous, fearful, and very difficult. The best way to approach these situations as a leader is to be open and honest about the struggle at the outset and then reinforce this throughout the workshops. The mix of cultures and expectations, if openly met and dealt with, is in itself a valuable learning experience. Over the years we have come to trust the process of this program to be helpful for all of the participants.

As coleaders of these workshops, we try to model what we are presenting. We question each other, as well as raise objections or differing points of view. We are courteous with each other and try to model critical learning and thinking. Many of our interactions are done for pedagogical purposes, but we also have genuine, specific divergent opinions about what is to be done or learned. An example of this is the use of the English language in workshops where English is not the primary language for some participants.

We do not avoid hot-button issues; we do point out that not knowing or not being certain is fine. To always have to be right is ultimately harmful. We model and therefore help the participants learn that working together is an important goal.

IN CONCLUSION

By the end of the three workshops, usually held over an eight- or nine-month period, a bond has developed among the participating group members. Evidence of this bond is seen in a concrete manner in longer meals and breaks, joyous laughter, and spirited small group sharing (even when individuals vehemently disagree but still continue to dialogue). Over the course of the sessions, significant life experiences are shared. There are moments of sadness as well as encouragement, desolation as well as consolation, not only in dealing with the complexity of cultural crossing but also with the reality of human frailty, vulnerability in ministry, and a myriad of personal issues.

The workshops offer a time to look back at life and ministry and see the grace of what has taken place over the years and in the engaging with others in the groups. How has God been at work in these processes?

We are convinced that the Holy Spirit in the Church is calling us to a new Pentecost. We, too, will see signs and wonders and we will marvel at the things that happen if we are open to the challenge of a universal Church. Multicultural is no longer geographic; it is local. And we are the local leaders who are being asked to step forward, listen to God's call, learn new skills, and practice the gospel. We pray that what God has begun, God will bring to completion.

FOR FURTHER REFLECTION

"Blessed are you who are poor, for yours is the kingdom of God.
"Blessed are you who are hungry now, for you will be filled.
"Blessed are you who weep now, for you will laugh.
"Blessed are you when people hate you, and when they exclude you, revile you, and defame you on account of the Son of Man.
"Rejoice in that day and leap for joy, for surely your reward is great in heaven." Luke 6:20–23

Handout 5a

Definitions of Culture

Culture. A system of inherited conceptions, expressed in symbolic forms by means of which human beings communicate, perpetuate, and develop their knowledge about and their attitudes toward life.

Culture. The study of culture includes the behaviors, technology, social organization, customs, and worldviews of people.

Culture. All that is nonbiological and socially transmitted in a society, patterns of behaviors and beliefs, as well as techniques for living and mastering the environment:
  • customs, information, skills (domestic and public) in peace and war, in science, art, and religion
  • the transmission of past experience to a new generation
  • capabilities and habits acquired by a person as a member of a society
  • every component of human existence: learned, structured, dynamic
  • natural and social adjustments of persons to environment
  • social knowledge passed to and through generations, language as a symbolic system being of major importance
  • a historical process
  • aspects, descriptive, historical, normative, psychological

Culture. The interior meanings, values, and identities that are shared by a group:
  • shared worldviews
  • the exterior material and institutional forms shared by a group
  • shared social organization and technology
  • organizes the chaos of experience
  • unconscious, ingrained assumptions

Definiciónes de Cultura

La cultura. Un sistema de ideas heredadas, expresado de manera simbólica por medio del cual los seres humanos se comunican, perpetuan y desarrollan su conocimiento acerca de y sus actitudes hacia la vida.

La cultura. El estudio de la cultura comprende el comportamiento/la conducta, la technología, la organización social, costumbres, y cosmovisión de un pueblo.

La cultura. Todo lo que no es transmitido biológica y socialmente en una sociedad; tanto patrones de conducta y creencias como tecnicas para vivir y dominar el ambiente:
- costumbres, información, destrezas (domesticas y publicas) en tiempos de paz y de guerra, en la ciencia, el arte y la religión
- la transmisión de la experiencia del pasado a las nuevas generaciónes
- capacidades y habitos adquiridos por una persona, como miembro de una sociedad
- todos los componentes de la existencia de la persona, los aprendidos, los estructurados, los dinámicos
- ajustes naturales y sociales de las personas a su entorno
- conocimiento social que pasa de un generación a otra del cual el lenguage es de primordial importancia
- un proceso histórico
- aspectos descriptivos, históricos, normativos, sicológicos

Cultura. Los significados internos, los valores y las identidades que comparte un grupo:
- cosmovisiónes compartidas
- las formas exteriores, materiales y institucionales compartidas por un grupo
- organización social y tecnología compartidas

Iceberg

language   fine arts   literature   drama   classical music
popular music   folk dancing   games   cooking   dress

notions of modesty   conceptions of beauty
ideals governing child raising   rules of who is related
worldview   people/animal relationships
patterns of superior/subordinate relationships   incentives to work
definitions of God, spirit, sin, religion   courtship/marriage practices
conceptions of justice   theory of disease   notions of leadership
tempo of life/work   patterns for decision making
conceptions of cleanliness   attitudes toward the dependent
problem-solving practices   social status mobility
eye-movement behavior
roles relative to age, sex, class, occupation, kinship
conversational patterns in various social contexts
conceptions of past and future
notions of logic and validity   definitions of insanity
friendship   family   stranger   insider   outsider
patterns of visual perception   body language
preferences for competition/cooperation
notions of child/adolescent/adult   social interaction rate
patterns for handling emotions/facial expressions
arrangements of physical space, and much, much more

Just as nine-tenths of an iceberg is out of sight (below the water line),
so is nine-tenths of culture hidden from our conscious awareness.

Handout 4b

Témpano

el idioma   las bellas artes   la literatura   el teatro   la música clásica
la música del pueblo   bailes folclóricos   los juegos
las comidas   el vestido

en qué consiste el recato
en qué consiste la belleza   los ideales que persigue
la educación de los hijos   la cosmovisión
las reglas que determinan el parentezco   cómo se trata a los animales
normas que gobiernan las relaciones entre superiores y subordinados
estímulos para el trabajo
definiciónes de Dios, el espiritual, el pecado, la religión
ideas sobre la justicia
custumbres acerca del noviazgo y el matrimonio
ideas sobre el liderazgo   ritmo de vida, de trabajo
modelos de toma de decisión   en qué consiste la limpieza
actitud hacia los inferiores/dependientes
teorías sobre las causas de las enfermedades
movilidad social   disciplina de los ojos
conducta social apropiado según la edad género, clase
ideas sobre el tiempo, el pasado y el futuro
patrones de percepción visual   lenguaje corporal
perferencis por competir/cooperar
ideas sobre la infancia, la adolescencia, la edad madura
proporción de intereacción social   ideas sobre la lógica y la validez
modelos para manejar las emociones   gestos/expresiones faciales
uso del espacio y muchisimo mas

Cómo solo la minima parte de un témpano está a la vista,
así también pasa con la cultura.
Una décima parte la podemos ver y ni siquiera
estamos conscientes del resto.